TAKE THE
ROBOT
out of the
human

Julian Boram

TAKE THE
ROBOT

out of the
human

**THE FIVE ESSENTIALS TO
THRIVE IN A NEW DIGITAL WORLD**

Cover design by Tom Howey.

Developmental and structural editing by Stephanie Boram. Content editing by Susan Gaigher. Proof editing by Rachael Churchill.

ISBN 978-1-7399252-0-8
Ebook ISBN: 978-1-7399252-1-5

This book is dedicated to my family, especially to my wife Gilda and our two children Stephanie and Natalie. I am so blessed to have their love and support, which encouraged and inspired me to research and write this book through a profoundly changing world.

CONTENTS

ACKNOWLEDGMENTS

Writing a book that spans business sectors, countries, and business models of all shapes and sizes has its challenges. Without the help from many experts, industry leaders, and pioneers around the world, this book would not have been possible. So, while it's difficult to name everyone who was so generous with their time, experience, and knowledge, I have listed a core few to show my appreciation and gratitude.

Ainslie van Onselen, Chief Executive Officer, CA ANZ; Rachel Grimes, Past President, IFAC; Helen Brand, Chief Executive, ACCA; Marise Maltman, Partner, Corporate Advisory, Deloitte, Australia; Ali Mehfooz, Global Head of Fund Services, AMP Capital, Australia; Michael Izza, Chief Executive, ICAEW; Steve Heathcote, Chief Executive Officer, PrimeGlobal; Rick Ellis, former Chief Executive Officer, CA ANZ, Non-Executive Director at The Icehouse, AUT Ventures Ltd and Chairman of Dexibit; Rhys Madoc, Global Chief Executive Officer, UHY Haines Norton, UK; Lynn Morrison, Partner, EY Australia; Susan Heart, Executive Dean of Business, Durham University; Brendan Sheehan, Chief Executive Officer, White Squires; Paula Kensington, Chief Executive Officer, LBD Group & Founder of PK CFO Conversations; Joseph Owolabi, Vice President, ACCA & Chief Executive Officer, Rubicola Consulting; Christophe Douche, Executive Director, Optus Macquarie Cyber Security Hub; Philomena Leung, Professor, Macquarie University; Michael Coughtrey, Managing Partner, UHY Haines Norton Sydney; Maggie McGhee, Executive Director, ACCA; Raymond Jack, Executive Director, Commercial ACCA and Alastair Robertson, Head of Continuous Improvement and Automation, Zurich UK.

I'd also like to acknowledge the myriad network groups, incubators and startup hubs, research and thought leadership initiatives that have assisted in developing the findings in this book, all of which I am very grateful for.

I would in particular like to acknowledge the great work being done by many of the professional bodies to help drive the future agenda, including IFAC, IAASB, IFRS, ACCA, ICAEW, PrimeGlobal, AICPA, CA ANZ, CPA, and SEMA, as well as consulting firms like BGC, McKinsey, KPMG, PWC, EY and Deloitte, and, of course, the World Economic Forum. I would also like to acknowledge the many universities and educators helping to build the leaders of tomorrow, such as Cambridge University, Harvard University, Oxford University, Durham University, Sydney University, and Macquarie University, including the Optus Macquarie University Cyber Security Hub, to name a few.

PREFACE

T here's really no escaping the digital and sustainable tidal waves that are threatening to wipe out unprepared businesses across the globe. Since the year 2000, over 50% of the traditional companies on the Fortune 500 list have disappeared, with other reputable businesses following in their footsteps. Why? Many ultimately failed to adapt and stay relevant. There are countless cases of established businesses that failed to innovate and followed the dodo bird down the path to extinction because they failed to meet customer expectations or evolve quickly enough to more sustainable business models. They also could have been simply outmanoeuvred by new, innovative competitors with better technology, nimbler operating models, or a more developed brand.

Some of these businesses you may recall, such as **Polaroid** – an instant film and polaroid camera business – which, at one point, had over 20,000 employees with three billion dollars in revenue, yet filed for bankruptcy in 2001 as it failed to successfully transition to digital. For decades, **Toys R Us** was one of the world's largest toy store chains for kids, yet vanished because it failed to evolve its business model and adapt to shifting consumer behaviour towards e-commerce. With continued competitive pressure from companies like Amazon, Walmart, and Target, it filed for bankruptcy in 2017, with many of its stores closing in 2018 around the world, and five billion dollars in long-term debt. Interestingly enough, in 2019, Toys R Us re-emerged as an online toy and clothing range owned by Tru Kids, Inc. with an entirely different e-commerce business model.

Then there was **Borders,** once a global book, movie, and music retailer, which went into liquidation because it failed to keep up with digital technology and changing consumer e-commerce needs. Borders backed the wrong horse and invested in physical real estate while shoppers were flocking to the internet and e-books. Exacerbated by competitor pressure from Amazon, iTunes, Netflix, and Kindle, Borders went the way of the dodo, filing for bankruptcy in 2011, listing around 1.3 billion dollars in debt.

Compaq Computers was one of the youngest ever Fortune 500 companies and was arguably one of the greatest David and Goliath stories in computer history pre-2000, yet it met its demise. It was eroded by more relevant competitors like Apple and IBM, as well as Dell, which grew rapidly with easy-to-buy online modular offerings, allowing customers the choice of more tailored options to build the specs on their PC or laptop that suited their needs. **Kodak** was once considered the world's largest photography, camera, and film company and is sometimes best known for delivering "analogue" photography, but after its long-standing dominance, Kodak, with over 140,000 employees, declared bankruptcy in 2012. It was unable to adapt its business model quickly enough, even though it was actually one of the first inventors of the digital camera. Kodak's "analogue" products became less relevant to its customers as technology improved. As a result, the century-old market was forced to sell off many of its patents and try to rebuild its business model exploring a diverse range of products such as smartphones, tablets, a photographer-orientated blockchain cryptocurrency and pharmaceuticals.

In addition, the COVID-19 pandemic has added another layer accelerating the need for businesses to shift gears rapidly to digital customer offerings, where some well-known businesses have had to file for bankruptcy as a result. **Hertz** filed in May 2020 with nearly eighteen billion US dollars in net debt on its balance sheet as tourism and business travel came to a standstill. **JCPenney,** an American department store chain, filed for bankruptcy in May 2020, burdened by 4.2 billion dollars in debt. **Virgin Australia**, an airline business co-founded by Richard Branson, filed for voluntary administration in April 2020. And the list goes on.

Today, business survival is predicated on an ability to stay relevant as the world turns digital, to stay abreast of new technology, sustainable value creation, and digital ways of doing things. This means being nimbler, able to improvise, adapt, and overcome the rapid challenges thrown at our feet faster than ever before.

INTRODUCTION

Change driven by new technology, or being outmanoeuvred by a competitor, is a dance that has been going on for centuries. But now, as the world rockets towards an AI-fuelled existence with cognitive automation, IoT, the metaverse, big data, and near-instant fulfilment, being relevant will be essential to stay in the race, where developing your "digital muscles" and building your Digital EQ will be necessary to be better equipped to ride the digital tidal waves. The Digital EQ model described in this book has been built with this in mind.

In a time when robots will take over millions of jobs across almost every industry, whether autonomously or working side-by-side with humans, backing yourself, your people, and investing in humans for the future will be the game changer.

This book has been written for business and finance professionals facing the daunting task of staying relevant and ahead of the digital curve. It has been designed to help people build the right digital muscles and resilience to thrive into the next decade. At its core, this means removing complexity and repetitive manual processes, and taking those robotic actions from people's lives. As tasks become automated, it will free you up to spend more time strengthening those quintessentially human qualities like empathy, relationship building, creative problem solving, and blue-sky thinking – all of which will be highly valued in the decades to come. By taking the robot out of the human and freeing up your time, your team, your executives, and your board, you will be able to focus more on value creation and heightened customer solutions. In doing so, you will build your Digital Emotional Quotient (Digital EQ) to help you better ride the digital wave.

Over the last eighteen months, I set out to speak with hundreds of professional business leaders, thought leaders, and pioneers to find the common areas of focus that drive their success. I have tried to look at a broader cross section in this book, speaking with universities, the Big 6 consulting firms, professional finance membership organisations, practices and corporations of various sizes, and some very interesting startups. From these, five key principles stand out that are identified and explored in this book that, when actioned in combination, help you build your Digital EQ. While there is no one size that fits all for where you, your teams, or your business are at on the digital transformation journey, my goal is to share this knowledge and to help you focus on areas that can make a difference to enable success and move from surviving to thriving.

While all of us are at different points along the digital curve and every business is at a different stage in its evolution, purposefully unshackling people from repetitive and mundane tasks that, until now, had to be done by humans, will free you up and enable you to develop broader value creation initiatives, new digital and future-focused skills, and agile mindsets and behaviours, and to build a stronger human focus.

The transformation loop never sleeps, and each industrial revolution cycle over the last 400 years has progressively become shorter and faster. No matter where you are on the transformation curve, constantly evolving technology advancements and global events are forcing more regular and more material pivots that we need to adapt to in order to survive. Our more interconnected IoT world is evolving. However, there is a way through, and it is squarely in your hands as to how you help shape the future for yourself, your teams, and your business.

HOW TO USE THIS BOOK

This book is written in three parts: why build Digital Muscle or Digital EQ, how to build it, and applying Digital EQ. I would suggest reading the book sequentially to begin with, and, of course, feel free to make notes in the margins or highlight any areas you feel are important to quickly refer back to.

The three parts are:

PART 1 – "Why build Digital Muscle or Digital EQ" looks at why it's essential to do something about this now and why, if you delay, you are at real risk of being left behind.

PART 2 – "How to build Digital EQ" goes into how you can start to build your digital muscles and Digital EQ using the five key pillars.

PART 3 – "Bring it all together: Applying your Digital EQ" looks at bringing it all together. Now that you're building Digital EQ, you can start to apply these principles to improve your business core using heightened ethics and change reaction management to deliver effective digital transformations.

CASE STUDIES AND SUMMARIES: Each chapter also has short case studies and/or commentary to highlight the chapter focus, as well as a short summary at the end of each part for quick reference.

THE EXERCISES: In each chapter, I have included short exercises designed to help you build digital muscles and get you thinking. The PDFs and more in-depth material can be downloaded from www.taketherobotoutofthehuman. com/exercises along with instructions. Type in SHAPE1 as the password to gain access. While every business is different, and every person is at a different stage on a digital transformation journey, these exercises should help you frame and focus your approach for you and your teams to get the best outcomes that are right for you.

PART 1

WHY BUILD DIGITAL MUSCLE OR DIGITAL EQ

Part 1 of this book explores the factors driving the urgency of why it's important to build your digital muscles or Digital EQ and stay relevant.

Chapter 1 looks at the convergent pressures driving the shifts and pivots that businesses are having to deal with. It explores the changing focus of the roles of finance and business professionals and what the transformation stages of digital maturity look like for businesses as they progress through the digital evolution stages. Finally, the chapter provides a CEO's perspective on some of the impacts of digital transformation, as well as some short exercises to help you identify where you and your business are on the transformation curve.

Chapter 2 looks at what the Digital EQ model is and the five core pillars that underpin it. It explores the shifts required to move from just surviving to thriving and finishes with a case study and a short exercise to help you identify your Digital EQ score.

The digital tide is well and truly rising up to our chins, and we all have to embrace building our digital muscles to survive and thrive in this new era.

CHAPTER 1

A CONVERGENCE –
NOWHERE TO HIDE

We live in highly disruptive times, and, whether you're ready or not, change is upon us and being driven by multiple converging pressures. According to a recent global report from McKinsey, the COVID-19 pandemic has radically transformed business and compressed five years of consumer and business digital adoption into a matter of weeks – a staggering reality to comprehend.

As if that wasn't enough, the race to achieve NetZero by 2050 and reverse the catastrophic effects of global warming has seen unprecedented impacts on businesses around the world. Many companies are grappling to keep up with the shifts and pivots required to develop more sustainable value creation business models that help make our world a better place. Recently, at COP26 in November 2021, Mark Carney, UN Special Envoy who chairs the Glasgow Financial Alliance for Net Zero, revealed that over 130 trillion dollars was required to help transform the economy to net zero, rising sharply from 5 trillion at the beginning of 2021.

Compounding these pressures are other global megatrends that are likely to cause disruptions across the business world well into the next decade. Whether it's more stringent and complex policies and regulations, economic volatility as a result of dynamic pressures in China and the US, how to better use and analyse data or deploying rapidly evolving automation technologies, the impacts are coming fast and strong. This pressure is further magnified by advanced customer behaviour being

<u>driven</u> by the new generation's appetite for far greater service levels than many businesses are currently geared to deliver. All of these influencing megatrends are colliding at the same time. Their potential energies combine, like many smaller waves merging together into one very large tidal wave with immense destructive force. These converging factors are accelerating the need for you, your teams, and your business to continuously pivot and evolve much faster than in previous times.

To overcome these material disruptions, we will need to do things a little differently than before. "IMPROVISE, ADAPT, and OVERCOME" is a phrase used by actor Clint Eastwood in the Hollywood movie *Heartbreak Ridge*, where he plays a US marine sergeant training a group of marines to fight for their lives, to change their behaviour and learn to improvise and overcome life-threatening obstacles, reinforcing a new mindset to overcome adversity.

While we're not strictly at war, being a business and finance professional today is a challenging role in disruptive times, getting more complex by the day. At the 2020 World Economic Forum in Davos, it was announced that around 50% of the world economy will be disrupted by the adaption of automation technologies and AI over the next ten years. These findings were made before the global impact of COVID-19, and it stands to reason the pandemic would only further exacerbate this estimate.

> *Over the next 10 years, 1.2 billion employees worldwide will be affected by the adaptation of automation technologies and AI. This is equal to 50% of the world economy and will disrupt $14.6 trillion US in wages.*
>
> —World Economic Forum 2020, Davos

This notion of AI disruption is further corroborated by the Harvard Business review predicting that three quarters of today's S&P 500 will be replaced by 2027. A further prediction can therefore be made that many current businesses will likely fail to stay relevant enough to meet customer expectations and will be replaced by more agile, AI, big data-driven alternatives more capable of meeting heightened customer needs. I recently met with the CEO of Chartered Accountants Australia and New Zealand (CA ANZ) and her view is that digital disruption is having significant impacts on the profession across the globe. She stated:

> *The sands are shifting across professions globally, and they need to be addressing this and steering into it: developing strategies – right now – and executing those strategies for the future. If they don't, they are at risk of being left behind.*
>
> —Ainslie van Onselen, Chief Executive Officer, CA ANZ

The bottom line is that it will be important to get into "digital shape" to be effective over the coming decades. Going through a digital value creation bootcamp, so to speak, will facilitate the development of behaviours, skills, and a renewed mindset that enable you to pivot more easily through constant change and build the skills to be more digitally effective as new technology is adopted and global events occur.

So, what's driving the convergence? The asset below shows key megatrends identified through workshops, interviews and research, that are colliding to fuel tidal waves across the business sphere.

ASSET 1.1: MEGATRENDS CONVERGE – DRIVING RAPID SHIFTS & PIVOTS

When these megatrends converge at once, it drives the rapid shifts and pivots that are rippling across the world. Many of these are self-evident; however, when they are all combined, the effects are magnified. A short explanation of each is provided below for context:

Global Events – COVID-19, global warming and volatile share markets: the economic and societal impacts of these events are rippling across the world with widespread consequences and ongoing implications. Businesses are forced to involuntarily pivot around global crisis events – on which COVID-19, global warming and the volatile share markets are three very material influences – and must quickly adapt or face becoming irrelevant.

Technology platforms changing rapidly: often, by the time you've set up a new system in a typical non-agile change management programme, it's obsolete before it can begin. Technology is changing too fast now for the more rigid, siloed, and slower-moving business models to keep up. Adapting to a more organic, fluid, and nimble model is what many businesses are exploring or are already shifting towards.

New breed of scalable, agile customer data-focused businesses: every week, new AI-fuelled businesses are appearing and this is happening across the full spectrum of industry sectors. Many of these are digitally enabled. They are not siloed, or legacy systems based and are far more agile with interconnected ecosystem partnerships across new technologies. Many have the ability to scale rapidly across digital channels.

A diverse pool of workers and thinkers: the new generations are here, with Gen Alpha on the way! Gen Y and Z are already becoming a material percentage of the workforce and with them comes a new way of thinking, working, and utilising digitally connected perspectives. They bring an aptitude for new technology and unencumbered acceptance of digital workers, bots, and AI. This new breed of workers and thinkers, when mixed with the older generations, opens up new challenges and opportunities.

Gig economy, employees, life balance and digital workforce: COVID-19 has accelerated the gig economy conversation. Many businesses and workers are now looking at how they can operate remotely and/or using consulting or contracting models. In addition to this, with the new digital workforce of bots becoming more commonplace, the talent pool and the shape of teams are rapidly changing and shifting.

Big data insight-driven innovation: this is the new fuel to power the modern business. Businesses need to be able to not only effectively capture and store vast amounts of data in the cloud, but also effectively analyse it, to provide up-to-date, real-time relevant insights that can drive customer satisfaction, customer innovation, and sustainable business value. Investment in the right systems, platforms, and people with the right skills will be required to fully realise the full value.

Shifting business models to stay relevant: as businesses grapple with converging megatrends, many are looking closely at their business models and the best way to stay relevant and to build a sustainable business. The business segments that are being impacted the hardest and the fastest are generally either driven by direct competitive pressure, where an agile competing business like Airbnb starts to steal market share from the traditional hotel segment, or as a result of one of the megatrends, like COVID-19, where rapid response is required for a business to change gears rapidly and become more digitally focused to stay solvent.

Heightened customer expectations: these are driven by the intuitive and more seamless, tailored experiences provided by digitally mature businesses like Amazon, Netflix, Airbnb, and Uber that are fuelling customer expectations and needs for service generally. Regardless of what business you're in, customers are expecting intuitive, good service. As such, businesses are looking more and more towards how they can effectively place the customer journey at the centre of their business model to improve the overall experience.

Businesses are all grappling with how to adapt to these shifts. In a recent discussion with the CEO of the Association of Chartered Certified Accountants

(ACCA), she expressed her view that rapid change has now become Business as Usual (BAU), where real shifts in mindset and accepting change are a constant and the new norm:

> *I used to get business reports that showed business investment over 3 years with benefits in 3–5 years. Those days are gone. Rapid change is now business as usual and the change piece is a constant, not a big thing that happens once a year. It's actually part of everyday business.*
>
> —Helen Brand, Chief Executive, ACCA

Being able to pivot, nimbly adapt, and lead change will be a vital skill to have as we move into the next digital decade.

Academics and universities are also endeavouring to conceptualise the rapidly developing skills gap being generated by the megatrend convergence. When I spoke with the Dean of Durham University's business faculty, her views on digital transformations were that:

> *It's a transformational world we're all in. With the fourth industrial revolution well and truly upon us, we have a role to play helping workers of the future and businesses, both locally and globally, through material business change.*
>
> —Susan Hart, Executive Dean of Business, Durham University

In the wake of COVID-19, many universities around the world are looking more closely at how to adapt their course structure, content, and delivery, which has been accelerated due to the need to socially distance and accommodate online learning requirements. A fresh approach and a new way of thinking about the future work-force is required to be better poised to embrace this change. Trying to balance a rich online learning experience and the physical brand value proposition has many universities looking carefully at the future. Many have already predeveloped incu-bators, accelerators, robotics programmes, and other new areas that help expand entrepreneurial behaviours and digital skillsets. However, doing this now digitally and retaining those decades or, in some cases, centuries of brand investment is the next challenge that universities are facing.

THE CONVERGENCE IS SHIFTING SKILLS AND ROLES

As the landscape changes, so too do the roles required to service it, whether you're managing ongoing regulatory changes that are not easily supported by business legacy systems or trying to unravel unconnected data to find business insights that drive profitable, sustainable growth. Perhaps you're grappling with disparate reporting engines and platforms that don't easily talk to one another, or the bigger questions of understanding how AI will impact your business and how to pay for it.

Beyond the core responsibilities of overseeing the finance functions, finance leaders today are also being asked to become strategic advisors to help drive sustainable change. One partner from Deloitte held the view that the role of the CFO was definitely shifting:

> *Historically, CFOs have been operators and stewards looking after the protection of assets and business effectiveness. But now, more and more, they need to be strategists and catalysts with a focus on business partnering, helping the board and business to navigate the business environment by providing the right information in a meaningful manner to allow them to make timely decisions.*
> —Marise Maltman, Partner, Corporate Advisory Deloitte Touche
> Tohmatsu

This shift in gears from being the quintessential stewards of a business will demand new skills, mindsets, behaviours, focus, and approaches to building partnerships across the business and wider ecosystems. As a modern finance leader, you're now being called on to enable strategy and partnerships, help to drive the vision, and become a proactive catalyst for change in the digital era. The CEO of Chartered Accountants Australia and New Zealand had a similar view and went further to say:

> *The introduction of accounting software has already helped the profession pivot from a rear view of analytics to a forward-looking strategic view. Rather than crunching numbers, they're*

now steering strategies, future forward ideas, partnerships and initiatives while AI picks up the rote data analysis that supports their decision-making.

—Ainslie van Onselen, Chief Executive Officer, CA ANZ

Many leaders I have spoken with have expressed concerns about staying relevant, what the roles look like, reskilling people, and being effective over the next digital decade. The Managing Partner of UHY Haines Norton Chartered Accountants Sydney said:

We're flat out running our business at 120 percent and it's a challenge to skill-up our people with new digital technology at the same time.

—Michael Coughtrey, Managing Partner,
UHY Haines Norton Chartered Accountants

Some of the most common questions raised are included in the asset below:

ASSET 1.2: COMMON COMMENTS ABOUT DIGITAL DISRUPTION

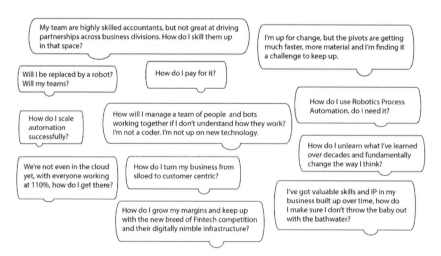

A recent report from the Association of Chartered Certified Accountants looks at the accountancy career in the 2020s and identifies five new zones of opportunity: assurance advocates, data navigators, business transformers, digital playmakers, and sustainability trailblazers. While some of these job titles do not exist yet, all of these are new directions that professional finance and businesspeople may need to consider when shifting from current roles to future roles, all of which will need new skills, behaviours, competencies, and mindsets.

THE TRANSFORMATION LOOP NEVER SLEEPS

Business transformations are not something that happen once and then you move onto something else; they're continuous, ongoing improvement that, like a loop, reoccurs as business, technology, data, customer needs, and markets evolve, and they are getting faster as technology enables more rapid change. While there is no one size that fits all as businesses and people are all at different stages of development with their digital evolution journey, digital business transformations can be categorised into three basic phases. The asset below shows the three phases that businesses travel along the digital transformation loop, as well as their resulting relationship with digital competency (or Digital EQ).

ASSET 1.3: THE DIGITAL TRANSFORMATION LOOP IS GETTING FASTER

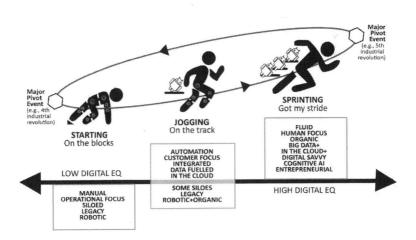

STARTING: ON THE BLOCKS – Businesses and people that are just starting their digital evolution journey are on the starting blocks, like a runner before the race starts. These businesses generally use older systems and approaches that worked for decades but are now under pressure to perform. They are typically aware that they need to do something but are not quite sure how to go about it. They often use multiple and complex legacy systems and more traditional approaches to operations. Upskilling and learning tends to be more intranet based and business models are less agile with often-rigid structures. The data tends to be more siloed and unconnected, and there is no clear, unified, customer-centric mandate. They tend to be process heavy and more risk averse, and people tend to be more bogged down by repetitive and manual tasks in their daily jobs. A global study recently conducted by ACCA showed around 65% of all businesses across all sectors are yet to implement any form of Robotic Process Automation (RPA) across their finance function. This type of business usually fits into the majority and tends to do things the way it always has, with little digital transformation or advancement at the present.

JOGGING: ON THE TRACK – Businesses that have progressed along the digital transformation curve and are dabbling with new technology, platforms, big data, and automation are on the track. You may feel like you've started the race, but there is a still a long way to go. These businesses typically have generally implemented some RPA projects, select cloud platform transitions, or API projects, or are working closer with third-party partnerships who have machine learning and/or RPA and AI support capabilities. ACCA recently researched a cross section of over 2,700 businesses globally, revealing that 46% of businesses were either trialling RPA or had partially or fully implemented RPA projects, with another 47% of businesses demonstrating a considerable lack of RPA skills and knowledge. For these businesses, some initiatives may have succeeded, and some may have failed, but the challenge seems to be how to scale the transformation across the entire business rather than a siloed project or division. The digital transformation strategy tends to be bottom up or side across, rather than unified and top down. Upskilling and learning is a blend of analogue with some continuous digital learning. These businesses generally embrace a more agile approach by utilising some automation amongst the large selection of repetitive, manual tasks.

SPRINTING: GOT MY STRIDE – These are businesses that are digitally mature and have found their stride, those that are already well advanced and leading the digital space. They possess an advanced digital understanding with big data analysis, customer insights, and utilisation at their core, such as the likes of Netflix, Uber, Airbnb, Google, Amazon, Tesla, as well as a stream of new nimble businesses entering markets across every sector. These businesses embody characteristics such as agility, data and customer-centric business models, and entrepreneurial behaviours. They are well connected with strong ecosystem partnerships and are generally using machine learning and cognitive systems to drive ongoing customer value, as well as encourage continuous loop learning. Teams and individuals alike within these businesses tend to be digital, customer focused, and big data savvy, with a curious and continuous learning mindset.

According to a recent Deloitte report, digital maturity will have a direct effect in driving financial impact. The report further stated that digitally mature organisations are nearly three times more likely than less digitally mature organisations to report net profit and revenue growth significantly above the average in their industry:

> *Digitally mature organisations are nearly three times more likely to report revenue growth significantly above their industry average.*
> —Deloitte report

So, the more digitally mature that the business, its teams, and its individuals are, the higher their Digital EQ and ability to effectively ride the digital wave. While Digital EQ means having a sound understanding and appreciation of the digital landscape and its rapidly evolving applications, it similarly calls for acute awareness of how you and the people around you are coping with the rapid digital change. As such, possessing well-rounded empathy helps you, your teams, executives, and boards to build stronger digital muscles and stay digitally relevant.

EXERCISE 1 – WHERE ARE YOU ON THE TRANSFORMATION CURVE?

To help kick-start your thinking process, visit www.taketherobotoutofthehuman.com/exercises and type in SHAPE1 as the password to identify areas you may want to more immediately focus on, download and fill in the scorecard. It identifies five dimensions – people, business, customers, value creation and entrepreneurial spirit – and should provide some quick insight to help you consider where you are on the curve and help move you forward.

A CHIEF EXECUTIVE'S PERSPECTIVE

When I recently met with the CEO of the Institute of Chartered Accountants in England and Wales, his view was that digital disruption will have significant impacts on the profession:

> *I think for accountancy professionals, the higher you are up the value chain, the better chance you have of making the transition to the more technological world we're going to find ourselves in. I think the jobs that are most ripe for disruption are those that can be replaced by machine learning, natural learning, and those tend to be repetitive, compliance-oriented, slightly mechanistic jobs, so if you take a finance department, perhaps the work of the purchase and sales ledger might be more easily replaced than that of the financial reporting, where there is more sophisticated judgement. That's not to say that those areas won't be immune from algorithmic intervention around professional judgement, but it won't come as quickly.*
>
> —Michael Izza, Chief Executive, ICAEW

There are many high-profile leaders at the forefront of the AI arena that have similar cautionary views on the impacts of AI. Elon Musk, Bill Gates, and the late Professor Stephen Hawking have all raised concerns about the impacts and potential threats of where the road to AI might take us.

When I spoke with the CEO of the Association of Chartered Certified Accountants, she took a different view, looking at the issue from a behavioural perspective:

> *I think the digital environment changes the market, people's expectation, and the customer. We, the older generation, get overanxious about the future because we don't change as quickly. We don't adapt to the digital environment as easily. However, with commitment and perseverance, new ways of doing things eventually become second nature.*
>
> —Helen Brand, Chief Executive, ACCA

When you've been used to doing something a certain way for a period of time, it's not always that easy to change your behaviour. Just because you're aware of something doesn't mean you can instantly apply it. It's a little like driving a car or riding a bike. It takes practice, commitment, and perseverance to get it right. Learning about new digital platforms, cognitive bots, and AI-fuelled big data analytics is no different. Once you have changed the behaviour, though, it becomes second nature.

The CEO of PrimeGlobal shared these views, and saw a rapidly changing landscape with professional accounting firms:

> *Professional service accounting firms used to be known for audit, accounting, and tax, with advisory and consultancy services emerging. That's totally breaking down now and as the variety of what firms do continues to evolve, they will look completely different within the next decade.*
>
> —Steve Heathcote, CEO, PrimeGlobal

However, while the impacts of COVID-19 are devastating, he saw that the profession is now in a privileged position, recognised now more than ever before as the trusted advisors that can help you in turbulent times:

We're in a really privileged position. Because COVID happened so fast, it accelerated the need for clients to reach out, which only strengthened our trusted advisor position. If things continued down the digital path, I'm not so sure that we would have ended up in the same place or adapted quickly enough.

—Steve Heathcote, CEO, PrimeGlobal

The CEO of Chartered Accountants Australia and New Zealand agreed with this view and went further to say:

There are huge opportunities ahead and professional accountants are in a really good place because they're known as trusted advisors, with a highly ethical lens, and are used to uniforming and analysing data, which will be one of the foundations for thriving in a digital future.

—Ainslie van Onselen, CEO, CA ANZ

As clients continue to turn to the businesses they trust, the pressure increases to continue to provide the right guidance in a digital world that enables clients to not only survive, but thrive. The former CEO of Chartered Accountants Australia and New Zealand, now a Non-Executive Director at The Icehouse, AUT Ventures Ltd and Chairman of Dexibit, advocated the need to embrace digital but ensure that your customers are at the centre of your business model:

What's critical is that existing businesses need to engage with the digital solutions in a strategic capacity to help them figure out how they embrace digital going forward. That capability needs to have a framework to understand the changing behaviour of their customers and figure out how to deliver relevant and valuable services.

—Rick Ellis, former CEO, CA ANZ, Chairman of Dexibit

The collective view is that things are changing rapidly and the need to adapt to a more fluid, digital world will become vital to ensuring businesses not only survive, but thrive into the next decade.

CHAPTER 2

USING DIGITAL EQ
TO NAVIGATE CHANGE

As businesses digitally transform to keep up with technology advancements and growing customer expectations, business models need to change. The skills and behaviours required to run these new modern businesses will be quite different to what they were yesterday or even today.

Think for a moment about working with teams of people and bots with varying degrees of intelligence and a new breed of technical know-how. These bots build reports overnight, ready for you in the morning when you log in. They can use machine learning to analyse trends and data, predict outcomes, and email you recommendations. The bots can read unstructured data or recognise things like images, photocopies, or photographs. These bots are highly intelligent and can learn. It's no longer just about managing people doing semiautomated and manual tasks. You'll now need to have an understanding of new technology and new platforms, and know how to manage future-focused teams of people and bots – a new digital workforce with new AI-fuelled platforms to enable big data-driven analytics drawing from a centrally-sourced, cloud-based data lake.

Imagine showing up for work (physically or remotely) and not having to deal with inefficient legacy systems that need manual intervention, reworking, or manual workarounds. Imagine running reports in real time, where customer and business data is not only accessible, transparent, and accurate, but fuels innovation and sustainable growth; where manual, mundane processes have been stripped out of people's job descriptions and you and your teams have been freed up to focus on more value creation opportunities that are less robotic.

The sobering part is that this technology is available now and indeed many businesses are using it to grow their brands. However, the challenge that many businesses face today when considering how to stay relevant is they often don't know where to start. To be able to improve or even rebuild a business model requires having the right people with the right skills who have more agile and future-focused behaviours to survive and thrive in this new digital era. This can be challenging if you're flat out trying to run a business through the shifts and pivots we discussed in Chapter 1. The good news is building the right digital skills, behaviours, and muscles (Digital EQ) can help you better navigate the digital tide. In this chapter, we'll look at:

- What the Digital EQ model is and the five core pillars that underpin it,
- Why building your Digital EQ is important, and
- How to build it more effectively, which is covered in more detail in the following chapters.

WHAT IS DIGITAL EQ?

Having a strong Digital EQ means building your digital muscles to be more relevant and poised to succeed in the coming digital decades. A simple definition for Digital EQ is your ability to effectively evolve in a rapidly changing digital world by having the right skills and continuous learning ability, a human 'customer' focus, an amplified value creation mindset in a more sustainably conscious world, broad-reaching partnerships across the business and wider ecosystems, and an entrepreneurial 'modern' spark to help adapt with agility and cope with rapid change, all filtered through a heightened ethical digital lens.

By empathising with people and motivating positive improvement through digital change, helping people collaborate with bots and new technology in a constantly transforming era – essentially strengthening the traits and behaviours that are quintessentially human to drive value and sustainable practices – you will be better poised to thrive in future state business models and more effectively manage digital business evolution.

Digital EQ is having a sound understanding and appreciation of the digital landscape, technologies, and evolving applications. It's about addressing skill gaps and a need for continuous learning, as well as being acutely aware of how you and the people around you are coping with the rapid digital change. To have Digital EQ is to have a well-rounded digital empathy to help yourself, your teams, executives, and boards stay relevant, helping people as they come to terms with this new reality: helping with anxieties such as, *Will I be replaced by a robot? Do I have the right skills needed to understand this new rapidly evolving technology and adapt to more nimble, agile business models that are more organic in nature?* When automation strips away repetitive, mundane manual tasks, it will be important to be able to take advantage of those traits that are inherently human, like blue sky thinking and creative problem solving.

Once you've strengthened your Digital EQ muscles, you will be far more effective when reviewing your strategy and business core with a sharper digital lens. In turn, you will be helping yourself and your teams shift behaviours and skills to build greater digital competency and to drive digital evolution action.

WHY BUILD YOUR DIGITAL EQ?

In Chapter 1, we discussed the convergence of megatrends all colliding, creating a digital tidal wave from which there is no escape. As a result, businesses are starting to go through a digital evolution which is transforming every industry, impacting the way we manage operations, people, technology, IT, finance, interacting with customers, and growing businesses sustainably. However, for many established companies, a vast amount of the work is being delivered through outdated and inefficient legacy systems and processes that aren't up to speed with the new, more agile digital business models needed to service growing consumer expectations.

Bots and humans working together is not science fiction or magic. It is happening now.

You might ask, *Is this is a problem I need to deal with right now? With lots on my plate in my day-to-day business life, surely I could push building stronger digital competency down the priority list? Surely, I can deal with this later.* The simple fact is that if you don't try to understand or appreciate new digital technologies, changing customer requirements, and ecosystem partnerships, there's a good chance you'll struggle to build trust with your teams. It doesn't mean you need to go out and learn how to code, but it will become increasingly harder to lead any transformation into a future state if you or your teams don't really understand the platform capabilities, pitfalls, or general principles. Further, any digital initiatives you deliver may well be unsustainable if you don't continuously build digital skills and capability, develop a customer focus across the business, build a value creation mindset underpinned by more nimble business models, as well as flex your entrepreneurial behaviours along the way.

Momentum and enthusiasm can quickly wane if your digital transformation initiative is treated simply as a one-off or siloed project and is not maintained, monitored, and continuously improved past its launch. The era of "continuous" is well and truly here.

However, while the need to change and adapt is evident, you might be wondering why you need to follow the Digital EQ model rather than jump straight into implementing initiatives. Well, according to a recent EY report that spans 20 countries, as many as 30 to 50% of initial RPA initiatives fail. While RPA is only one plank in a digital transformation, it's often a good indicator of a business's intent to transform to a more effective business model. The report went on to say that the high failure rate often isn't a reflection of the technology itself, and that there are some common issues in failed RPA projects that will often prevent an organisation from delivering on the promise.

There are numerous examples of digital transformations or automation projects that have delivered average results or have failed in some way. The reasons given vary depending on the digital maturity of the business, the leaders, and the individuals involved, but, at the centre, the common theme is almost always that the principles of Digital EQ have not been applied. You may be familiar with or have heard of some of these reasons yourself, such as:

ASSET 2.1: A FEW REASONS FOR FAILURE WITH DIGITAL TRANSFORMATIONS

Often when digital programmes are conducted as small one-off initiatives, they are at risk without the proper focus, strategy, and planning. Where the exec, board, and cross-functional commitment has not been established, coupled with a cursory or non-robust digital transformation strategy that is driven from the top, sides, and bottom, businesses can run the risk of delivering a failed programme.

It's a little like building a house. If you don't have the right plans developed, using knowledgeable engineers to assess footings, and architects to design the structure and orientation, the house is likely to, at best, leak or, at worst, fall down over time.

A recent Deloitte report explored the correlation between benefits and digital maturity, finding that a higher level of digital maturity delivers better financial performance. About half the companies in their survey exhibiting higher digital maturity reported their net profit margin and revenues were significantly higher than the industry average, believing that digitally mature organisations could "identify and seize opportunities, develop new revenue streams, respond with more agility to customer market demands, and operate with greater efficiency." So, in effect, the greater your Digital EQ, the greater depth of knowledge you have to more effectively thrive in future-state, agile organisations; and with greater digital skills and understanding, the more effective any digital transformation will be.

HOW TO BUILD DIGITAL EQ AND NAVIGATE CHANGE

We're all at different stages with different requirements as we move along the digital transformation curve. There is no one-size-fits-all solution; however, continuous learning will be one of the key dimensions. A recent McKinsey report looking at global workforce skills found that, from a survey of over 3,000 business leaders across the western globe, continuous learning is viewed as the most important element for a changing workforce.

Building Digital EQ is a long-term, ongoing proposition and doesn't stop once you've learned about the latest new platform, tools, or automated process. The way we need to learn has changed; ongoing learning, unlearning, and re-learning is going to become the new norm in this fast-paced digital world.

The Digital EQ model below has been built after working and speaking with hundreds of professional business leaders, professional accountants, CEOs, universities, partners, and pioneers, where five common pillars emerge. Building strength in these core areas will help you become more relevant in the coming decade. The model is summarised in the asset below.

ASSET 2.2: BUILDING YOUR DIGITAL EQ TO HELP SHAPE YOUR FUTURE

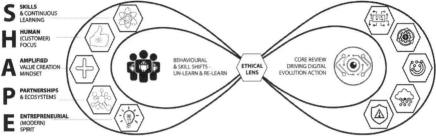

It's probably no surprise that the Digital EQ model above is in the shape of an infinity loop, as it reflects the digital transformation or evolution process, which is continuous. As we're all trying to get our heads around the implications of the fourth industrial revolution, the fallout of COVID-19, and the uncharted fifth industrial revolution just around the corner, there is a continuous need to review, assess, adapt, and overcome as things rapidly and continuously change. The model has two distinct sides, both of which continuously flow through a heightened ethical lens.

BEHAVIOURS AND SKILLS TO BUILD YOUR DIGITAL EQ: On the left side of the infinity loop sit the five core behavioural and skills pillars that help SHAPE your digital future. Below is a summary of the five core pillars.

1.   **SKILLS AND CONTINUOUS LEARNING**: Develop skills and behaviours to deal with emerging new technologies that fit better with evolving business models on the road to AI. With humans and bots as the new face of business workforce, developing the right forward-looking skills to ride this new digital wave will be essential. There will be a great deal of change management occurring across organisations, so having a good understanding of the right skills and behaviours needed as new technology is deployed is paramount to business sustainability.

2.   **HUMAN (CUSTOMER) FOCUS**: Take a customer focus to ensure your customer sits at the centre of your business, with humans in the loop for AI and automation. It doesn't matter what business you are in – with agile, digital-savvy businesses like Uber, Airbnb, Netflix, and so

many others offering great, data-fuelled customer experiences, customers today expect transactions with your business to be intuitive, uncomplicated, easy, and effective. A bad customer experience can destroy your brand overnight. So, it will be important to look at how you're dealing with your customers through a customer-centric lens in order to stay relevant – to adopt a dynamic customer-focused approach and ideally have consistent customer-focused KPIs across the whole business, driving everyone to work together.

3. **AMPLIFIED VALUE CREATION MINDSET:** For a world with changing values, think more broadly about deriving sustainable, community and environmental value as well as shareholder return has become an urgent focus for the business world. Following COP26 in November 2021, the general view was that current policies and global strategies to drive down NetZero emissions by 2050 will fail to hit the desired 1.5% target for CO_2 emissions necessary to save our planet. The current projected trajectory is double that, which means unless we can rapidly accelerate our efforts to reduce CO_2 emissions in this next decade, we will pass the point of being able to reverse the damage. As a result, being able to develop sustainable business models, products and services that create sustainable value will be a major challenge for businesses over the next decade.

4. **PARTNERSHIPS AND ECOSYSTEMS:** Looking broader and thinking outside the box at different business models and opportunities will open up areas you may not have even considered. This can take the form of partnering with organisations that fill a customer journey gap, data management gap, or skills and knowledge gap, like startups or incubators to draw on nimble and more agile business models, helping to expand your knowledge pool by extension.

5. **ENTREPRENEURIAL (MODERN) SPIRIT:** This doesn't mean you need to own a startup or take extraordinary risks, but adopting a modern entrepreneurial spirit will allow a more agile and fluid approach to business operations. This means thinking more nimbly and commercially, where you are developing evidence and a proof-of-concept approach

with clear business cases to demonstrate early success, testing and re-testing with a nimble, flat and transparent style of engagement across multiple teams, breaking down silos to drive collaboration and deliver centralised results. Be open to changes in direction and pivots.

I can guess what you might be thinking. We are not all billionaire CEOs like Jeff Bezos, Steve Jobs, Walt Disney, Elon Musk, Mark Zuckerberg, or Jack Ma. The good news is that entrepreneurial behaviour is not just about being a standout CEO that builds successful billion-dollar companies. Modern-day entrepreneurial behaviours are being exhibited by people every day – displaying courage, testing and re-testing to improve the outcomes, applying a style of engagement across teams that drives collaboration, and developing clear business cases with a strong proof of concept that demonstrates success. These are all elements of entrepreneurial behaviour that can be learned.

It's worth mentioning that this book focuses more on the left-hand side of the model to build your Digital EQ. These pillars are explored more fully later in Part 2.

BUSINESS CORE REVIEW DRIVING DIGITAL EVOLUTION ACTION: On the right-hand side of the infinity loop sit the business core pillars. Once you've developed a stronger Digital EQ, you can more effectively review the core of your business or functional area. The key is to now apply a more advanced digital awareness and take action to enhance and evolve your strategies as your business evolves. This is explored more fully in Part 3.

Once you've built stronger digital muscle and have developed the right behavioural and skill shifts to build your Digital EQ, it will be important to take a fresh look at all the core business pillars with an enhanced digital and ethical lens to ensure you, your teams, and your business will thrive over the next decade. The specific areas in your business core may vary, depending on your area of expertise.

It's about ensuring the business has robust controls, sustainable revenue, and a sustainable business strategy embracing the fourth industrial revolution. The business core review might include ensuring a fluid strategy and revised measurement are developed in a new, shifting digital environment. Reviewing the business model allows you to understand how to best deliver the transformation strategy effectively, ensuring technical processes and infrastructure readiness are in place as the business evolves through to digital maturity. It also ensures there is a clear data access and digital agility strategy to cope with the business evolution as it becomes a nimbler, customer-centric business, and, most importantly, to ensure that ethics and compliance are at the heart of the approach.

It's also about focusing on the end-to-end customer journey, the new heightened customer experience, brand evolution as the business becomes more agile, sales through new digital channels, customer engagement channels, and marketing levers to drive customer satisfaction. It's about ensuring that there is a fluid strategy aligning with the business transformation or evolution strategy, adapting and devising effective marketing models to support newly evolving Martech platforms and solutions to ensure they align and emulate consistent brand values with the right level of empathy, working as one team collaboratively with finance and technology divisions to ensure data accuracy, and implementing a clear segmentation strategy to drive cognitive and insightful analytics, along with reviewing legal and data compliance exposure of all brand-aligned communications and content.

The dynamics of reviewing your core business model may vary depending on whether you're reviewing a whole-business strategy, a strategy for part of the business such as marketing or information technology, or a people strategy. The model is flexible so it can be applied across a business or a specific division. It's up to you how you'd like to use it.

Regardless of where you are on your digital transformation journey – whether you're at the start, on the track, or already have your digital stride where you're delivering a cybersecurity review, moving platforms into the cloud, or implementing bots across divisions – the principles of building Digital EQ will help you become more effective in this digital era and ride the digital wave.

It's also essential to note that a heightened ethical lens has been set as a central filter that should be applied to everything. As cognitive algorithms become more the norm, ensuring the right ethics are applied to coding, the automated business rules, and cognitive unassisted automation enhancements, the management of bots and so on will be even more important to get right.

Once you take the robot out of the human, removing repetitive and laborious manual tasks, the shackles are off to focus on value creation and building your Digital EQ across the five key dimensions. As you develop these, you will become more capable and effective at reviewing your core business focus with a digital and ethical lens to build a more sustainable business for the future.

After you've strengthened your Digital EQ muscles, you will be far more effective when reviewing your strategy and business core with a sharper digital lens. In turn, you will be helping yourself and your teams shift behaviours and skills to build greater digital competency and to drive digital evolution action.

If you're finding it difficult to know where to start, how to decipher the hype and wade through the jargon, you're definitely not alone. The key is to develop a clear strategy, accepting that it's a long-term strategy and you need to be in for the long haul. Then start with small shifts in behaviour, mindset, focus, partnerships, and skills, with a continuous learning approach. This signifies an inevitable shift from how you used to do things, to a more fluid, continuously evolving future state for you and your business going forward.

The value framework asset below was developed based on common themes that are practised by business leaders and pioneers, demonstrating that as you build Digital EQ, your ability to improve from just surviving in a digital world to actually thriving accelerates as you gain proficiency. It's not rocket science, but the more you know, understand, and practise, the better you become. The key to progress is driven across the five key dimensions: Skills, Focus, Mindset, Relationships, and Behaviours.

ASSET 2.3: THE DIGITAL EQ VALUE MODEL – CORE SHIFTS

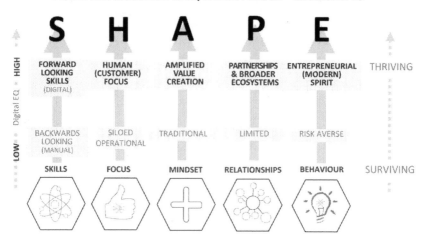

Shifting from just surviving with a low Digital EQ to a high Digital EQ will allow you to thrive in today's digital world. While it depends on where you are along the digital transformation curve and how digitally mature your business is, once you have begun to strengthen your Digital EQ, you will have greater ability to improve your business model using a sharper digital lens and understand how best to adapt and optimise for the future.

As there is typically no crystal ball that clearly roadmaps the way to a definitive digital transformation, feeling your way in the most informed manner possible really plays into strong leadership and the need for courage. In our Multi Billion Dollar Funds Management case study example below, they were at the start of their digital transformation journey, without any real definitive RPA runs on the board. So, there is a certain amount of test and re-test required, which may not immediately fit comfortably with risk profiles and more traditional business model approaches. Other core areas to consider included technical and infrastructure readiness, data access and organisational digital agility, heightened ethics and compliance, and fluid strategy and measurement. However, we cover this in more detail in Chapter 8.

EXERCISE 2 - RATE YOUR DIGITAL EQ - SCORE CARD

Go to www.taketherobotoutofthehuman.com/exercises and type in SHAPE1 as the password to download this short exercise that should help you see where you are on the Digital EQ scale and provide some insights around the areas you need to focus and build upon. Once you're done, you can also use this score card for your teams, executive, board, broader business, and partners. In the rest of Part 2 of this book, we go into more detail for each of the five areas. So, read on as we unpack these for you one at a time.

CASE STUDY – MULTI-BILLION-DOLLAR FUNDS MANAGEMENT BUSINESS

Applying the SHAPE Principles

A multibillion-dollar funds management company I recently did some work with kick-started their digital transformation journey in the Finance Department by implementing a successful Robotics Process Automation (RPA) project in the fees and billing team to achieve material results. Ali Mehfooz, the Global Head of Funds Management leading the initiative, did this by applying the five core principles of Digital EQ.

Prior to this RPA initiative, Ali and his team were frustrated with having to perform ongoing, repetitive, and time-consuming tasks, as well as having to manage multiple, disparate reporting engines and accounting platforms that didn't easily talk to one another when trying to unravel unconnected data. The added threat of margin erosion through competitive pressure was also a key concern, as well as customer experience being merely acceptable rather than optimal. There was simply no time for value creation work amongst the burden of legacy infrastructure. He also had the challenge of trying to motivate a demotivated finance team with relatively low engagement scores – around 50% overall across a variety of measures. The primary driver was that they had expectations of potentially losing their jobs as part the automation programme.

Ali was acutely aware that many businesses were contemplating AI solutions to stay relevant and after reviewing various options, he was convinced that implementing an RPA initiative would deliver the best solution to kick-start the journey. However, he still needed to convince his executives, his team, and his peers that the project was worth the disruption, effort, and risk.

At this time, the business was in the "STARTING" phase of their digital transformation journey and there was no company-wide digital transformation strategy in place. Initially, like with many new ideas, there was some resistance from the business leadership and the wider teams. However, this did not stop Ali, who applied Digital EQ principles to drive tangible results. By applying an entrepreneurial spirit and demonstrating courage, conviction, and strong leadership, he forged ahead with a clear strategy.

Ali applied Digital EQ principles and took the bull by the horns. He developed a sound business case and produced an effective proof of concept to demonstrate value and build confidence. The initiative was HUMAN (CUSTOMER) FOCUSED and designed to alleviate customer issues, delivering a great result by making the process far smoother and removing annoying errors and delays. The processes were also built with humans in the loop and designed to be sustainable and fit for automation. He developed new SKILLS AND CONTINUOUS-LEARNING, educating himself first and then helping to skill up his team. With digital empathy, he spent time effectively bringing his teams along the journey, subsequently building their trust. By being able to empathise with their digital dilemmas, he was able to show them tangible benefits of working collaboratively with bots and no longer having to produce reams of spreadsheets, manually enter data into legacy systems, and physically do mundane tasks that a bot could easily do overnight to have ready to review in the morning.

By using an AMPLIFIED VALUE CREATION MINDSET, he sought to build value that helped his clients, and also removed repetitive manual tasks prone to human error and developed new, more sustainable processes that worked more effectively with a bot and paperless environment. He did not simply replicate the previous processes, as they were not geared to work in an automated environment, but instead used design thinking to rebuild the business process. He developed PARTNERSHIPS AND ECOSYSTEMS, both externally with new platform providers like Automation Anywhere and by building connections across divisions, breaking down more traditional siloes and driving far more unity and collaboration. He developed broader ecosystem partnerships with RPA technology providers and even brought in fresh-thinking university graduates to help disrupt the process mapping to ensure there was a fresh customer-centric perspective. He broke down the cross-divisional siloes and encouraged cross-divisional teams working together to build a richer picture and solution. Finally, he adopted ENTREPRENEURIAL MODERN BEHAVIOUR with certainty and conviction, and he was able to build trust with the executives and wider teams based on demonstration and fact. His team trusted that he would redefine their job descriptions, ultimately taking the robot out of the human, and free them up to spend more time on more value creation initiatives.

Overall, he delivered a highly effective robotics process automation initiative with very positive outcomes. As a result, he forged his own path, was promoted, and was given more responsibility with larger teams (people and bots alike) to oversee. He rapidly improved his team morale and skills, drove incremental revenues, and delivered a better customer experience with significantly fewer errors and time delays for billing queries.

THE RESULT was over six thousand hours of unwanted repetitive work successfully removed across the teams to allow more value creation work, and millions of dollars in incremental revenue in a relatively short period by reducing the time taken for the fees and billing cycles through automation. He also established a centre of excellence (CoE) to help drive ongoing improvements. But most importantly, he put his people first, redesigned their job descriptions, and engaged them through the process. As a result, he shifted the staff engagement scores from 50% to over 90% throughout the course of the initiative. He did this by building and applying Digital EQ, showing people the benefits and opening up to more value creation opportunities.

SUMMARY: PART 1

CHAPTER 1 - A CONVERGENCE - NOWHERE TO HIDE

Rapid change is upon us. However, considering these key principles driving the need to digitally transform will help prepare your thinking for the road ahead to developing your Digital EQ.

A CONVERGENCE - DRIVING MATERIAL CHANGE: There are a number of factors colliding that are driving rapid change, from global crisis events, gig economy and digital workers, to new technology, big data-driven, customer-focused businesses, and new ecosystem-driven platforms. You need to consider these megatrends as you develop your strategy moving forwards.

THE CONVERGENCE IS SHIFTING SKILLS AND ROLES: As a result of megatrend convergence, the roles for the business and finance profession are shifting away from the tradition-trusted steward to more strategic, transformational, and partnership-focused. You need to consider where your business is heading, its strategy, and what role you want to create for you and your teams.

THE TRANSFORMATION LOOP NEVER SLEEPS: The transformation loop is an ongoing evolution. Consider where you are on the curve to help get a reality check and start planning the road ahead.

CHAPTER 2: USING DIGITAL EQ TO NAVIGATE CHANGE

A definition of Digital EQ is *your ability to effectively evolve in a rapidly changing digital world by taking the robot out of the human and having the right human "soft skills" – amplified value creation* **mindset**, *human (customer) focus, entrepreneurial modern* **behaviours**, **skills** *and continuous learning, partnership and ecosystem-building* **relationships** *– and by empathising and motivating positive improvement through digital change. It is helping people collaborate with bots and new technology in a constantly transforming era and strengthening those traits and behaviours that are quintessentially human to drive value and sustainable practices.*

The multibillion-dollar funds management case study is a good example of what happens when you put the core elements of Digital EQ into practice at a very real and tangible level. It's something that can be implemented immediately within the area of your control.

BUILD YOUR DIGITAL EQ: Developing digitally focused behaviours, focus, skills, mindsets, and partnerships will help build your digital capability and drive the right change management across your teams and business. Having a better understanding of how to lead in a digital world will give you more credibility as a leader and provide more reasons for teams to want to work with you. Don't forget to build your digital brand to demonstrate ongoing value in today's world.

The answer to "**How do I change?**" is to proactively shift along the five key dimensions of Digital EQ. By really being clear on your **why**, then building your Digital EQ muscles, you will be more effective and more relevant, and will better ride the digital wave. The five key shifts:

1. **SKILLS AND CONTINUOUS LEARNING:** shift from retro and ad-hoc learning to developing continuous skills and behaviours that better deal with emerging, new technologies

2. **HUMAN (CUSTOMER) FOCUS:** shift from operationally focused to customers first, as well as ensuring that humans are in the loop for AI initiatives

3. **AMPLIFIED VALUE CREATION MINDSET:** shift from traditional and revenue focused to broader sustainable value.

4. **PARTNERSHIPS AND ECOSYSTEMS:** shift from narrow and siloed to broader ecosystems and partnerships

5. **ENTREPRENEURIAL (MODERN) SPIRIT:** shift from risk-averse, manual, and inward-focused to agile with an entrepreneurial spirit

But above all, take the robot out of the human and build those skills and behaviours where humans differentiate themselves from machines and thrive.

SOME KEY PRINCIPLES TO HELP YOU GET STARTED

GET MOVING: Don't get left at the back of the pack. Start now. Regardless of whether your teams have digital transformation upskill programmes in place or they're around the corner, don't put it off. Start looking at what you need to do now to get ahead of the curve and ride the digital wave.

GET REAL: Assess where you're at. Be honest and assess the gaps. Understand where the skills gaps are for yourself, your teams, and your business to uphold the right level of professional standards and continue to build trust with customers and the community.

GET RELEVANT: Embrace constant learning. The digital era is here, whether you're ready or not. For you, your team, your board, and your business to become more valuable, employable, and effective, staying up-to-date and relevant will be fundamental.

GET AGILE: Fluid and constant change is the new BAU. With the speed that technologies change, transforming from one way of doing business to a new one involves continuous, nimble change management. "IMPROVISE, ADAPT, OVERCOME."

GET SUSTAINABLE: Developing sustainable business practices, models, teams, and processes will be important to ensure the new digital strategy you put into place doesn't fall over because you've simply replicated the human version. As the world becomes more digital, we'll all need to keep up.

PART 2

HOW TO BUILD YOUR DIGITAL EQ

Part 2 of this book explores the SHAPE model and shows you how to build your Digital Emotional Quotient (Digital EQ) and stay relevant in the next digital decade. Most of us are familiar with the term IQ, which is a measure of someone's intelligence, whereas EQ measures someone's emotional intelligence. Digital EQ is a measure of someone's digital emotional intelligence, which is designed to help you better navigate the digital disruption flowing from the fourth industrial revolution and global events forcing profound changes to our lives and businesses.

This part looks at HOW to build your Digital EQ by applying five core principles that many thought leaders and pioneers use today. The following chapters unpack the five core pillars to help you **SHAPE** your digital future.

1. **SKILLS AND CONTINUOUS LEARNING:** developing continuous learning skills and behaviours to deal with rapidly evolving technologies

2. **HUMAN (CUSTOMER) FOCUS:** applying a customer-centric lens to your business, with humans built into the loop for AI and automation initiatives

3. **AMPLIFIED VALUE CREATION MINDSET**: taking a more sustainable and community view of value for a world with changing values

4. **PARTNERSHIP AND ECOSYSTEMS:** partnering across your business and wider ecosystems to broaden your value proposition

5. **ENTREPRENEURIAL (MODERN) SPIRIT**: taking a modern agile entrepreneurial approach to adapt to the rapid shifts and pivots

When these are applied together, they will help you to become more relevant, build stronger and more sustainable digital muscles, and develop strategies to keep up with rapid change.

When you take the robot out of the human and free people up, you can replace these repetitive, time-consuming tasks with dynamic, agile, value-creation- and customer-focused, forward-looking behaviours, freeing you up to build the necessary core digital aptitude to help SHAPE your digital future.

CHAPTER 3

SKILLS AND CONTINUOUS LEARNING

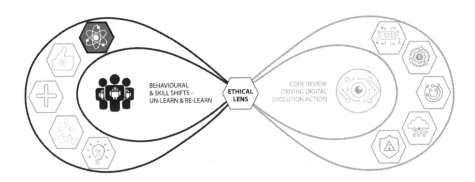

With the rapid changes in technology, remaining relevant in the coming decades will require unlearning old ways and developing more continuous learning habits and skills to help us stay ahead of the curve. While this may sound like something you could put on the back burner for the time being, according to the leaders and pioneers I've spoken with, it really isn't. To keep up and get ahead will require a different approach to learning. At the 2020 World Economic Forum in Davos, it was discussed that the world will need to reskill more than a billion people over the next decade.

As jobs are transformed by the technologies of the fourth Industrial Revolution, we need to reskill more than one billion people by 2030.

—2020 World Economic Forum, Davos

This is why PricewaterhouseCoopers (PWC) recently invested over a billion dollars in re-training and digitally upskilling their global workforce. Similarly, Walmart invested over $2 billion in wages and training to help teach employees soft skills, Amazon recently pledged $700 million to retrain 100,000 employees for higher-skilled jobs in technology, and JPMorgan Chase committed $350 million over a five-year period to develop technical skills that are in high demand. What these organisations have in common is the commitment to invest in their people to develop the right skills needed to thrive in the coming digital decade.

Right now, businesses are trying to remain relevant. One of the many challenges they face is having the right number of skilled people with the right capabilities, as well as the right human-based, softer skills like creative thinking, relationship building, communication, digital empathy, and blue-sky thinking. They need to evolve from outdated learning skills, older mindsets, and habits to better match a new automated, AI-fuelled world. This means embracing a different way of operating and thinking, which can be a challenging task.

The good news is that building continuous learning skills and habits can quite easily be developed, even if you're not used to continuous learning. In this chapter, we explore:

- what continuous learning skills are?
- why you need to put your people first in a digital world?
- how developing these skills will help you become more relevant.

We'll also dive into how you can start to develop the right continuous learning skills, self-awareness, digital empathy, and relationships to build your own Digital EQ.

WHAT ARE CONTINUOUS LEARNING SKILLS?

Continuous learning skills refers to the sustainable ability to more regularly and rapidly learn new information and behaviours to keep up with change. For some who are already curious and comfortable with digital learning, developing this ability may be simple. For others with different learning styles and behaviours, for whom continuous learning has not been a necessity, this may mean developing new, sustainable habits and making them a more regular part of their daily lives.

Developing continuous learning skills requires a number of factors to build the right habits and make them stick. It means fostering a curiosity and interest to learn more to build your knowledge and become the best you can be. This may involve changing your learning style from being a less active learner to a continuous learner as part of your regular daily or weekly routine, no matter how large or small the information is you consume. It means being open to unlearning old habits and re-learning new ones in a world where information is more readily available than at any other time in the history of humanity. Finally, it's about having a balanced, human focus in a digital environment. By that, I mean building your core human skills like communication, relationship building, creative thinking, and building digital empathy around new technology to help others work through this evolving digital world.

At the 2020 World Economic Forum in Davos, Bob Moritz, PWC's global chairperson, outlined their multibillion-dollar investment in developing the continuous learning skills of their 275,000 staff. He has a vested interest in the personal success of his staff, stating that "if people are the change agents, you need to give them the right digital tools and skills necessary to do the job." This commitment involved developing a mobile app to help his staff better understand their digital fitness. The app assesses their preferred learning styles and provides a tailored digital fitness plan for them which not only helped increase their knowledge, but also helped change learning behaviour to a more agile and regular habit. PWC recognises the vital importance of helping their employees build robust digital muscles to adapt to the new digital era. But they did not just focus on technical knowledge, they included more human "soft skills" as well. As a result, the digital app provided continuous, easily digestible learning material on new digital technology, platforms, and practices. Part of this included developing KPIs that were gamified and helped to drive the right behavioural shifts.

Other global consulting firm I have spoken with also share this kind of view. Lynn Morrison, Partner at Ernst & Young (EY), said:

I believe you need to put people first, and, in a digital age, soft skills need to be a focus.

—Lynn Morrison, Partner, Ernst & Young

As automation and AI really start to pick up momentum, we need to strengthen our uniquely human capabilities, or soft skills. In so doing, we will be able to thrive and create exponential value within a technologically driven world, while machines and algorithms pick up the monotonous work that should be automated.

WHY DEVELOP THESE SKILLS?

Imagine if you started work one morning and all of those repetitive, labour-intensive manual tasks were already done for you. Imagine those spreadsheets and reports were populated by autonomous bots working tirelessly through the night. Imagine a centralised and integrated master dashboard providing key insights to your business or division. That these were all done by algorithms and cognitive learning bots that had already analysed and optimised your customer and business data, providing rich insights. Imagine collecting information from the whole organisation without the usual divisional silo barriers, and it being all visible in one place. Your reports are ready for final review, ready to be automatically deployed on emails or collaboration platforms once you've approved the content. Depending on your specific role, up to 50% of your current workload could now be freed up before your day has even begun. As your team or colleagues start to consist more and more of both people with a diverse range of learning styles and bots – all working together physically or virtually – a key part of your role into the future will be to lead, influence, and/or motivate this new modern team.

Most of us are facing similar challenges with a need to skill up to keep up with rapidly shifting technologies, evolving business models, and broadening skill gaps, but at the same time, juggling the need to deliver our business objectives, KPIs, and outcomes. However, it's imperative to take the bull by the horns and start looking at how you can shift into a more continuous, agile learning behaviour now. Don't wait for your board, CEO, executive, or manager to start developing forward-looking skills programmes that continuously build your digital muscles as technology evolves.

You might be asking, "Can't I just attend that three-day virtual conference, or can't I just simply follow the internal HR programme for personal development?" The short answer is, it's just not enough. We need to take charge of our own destiny. The convergence highlighted in Chapter 1 is creating shock waves across businesses globally. Material pivots and shifts are becoming the norm, disrupting the way we've done business and the shape of business into the future so there is literally nowhere to hide. So, developing forward-looking skills and putting people first will be key to avoid going the way of the dodo. Not surprisingly, a recent McKinsey Global Institute article raised an important fact:

> *By 2030, 30–40% of all workers in developed countries may need to move into new occupations or at least upgrade their skillset significantly.*
>
> —McKinsey Global Institute 2020

Building Digital EQ is a long-term, ongoing proposition and doesn't stop once you've learned about the latest new platform, tools, or automated process. The way we need to learn has changed. Mirroring this sentiment, the World Economic Forum Future of Jobs report stated that:

> *By 2022, everyone will need an extra 101 days of learning to stay relevant in their roles.*
>
> —World Economic Forum 2020, Davos

A well-known truth about humans is that many of us don't really like change. So, how do you get people who are used to working a particular way to start collaborating and working with bots, new technology platforms, and new streamlined processes? How do you get people who are comfortable working one way, and probably have been doing so for a long time, to change their behaviour, skills, focus, and mindset?

HOW DO I DEVELOP CONTINUOUS LEARNING SKILLS?

We all have our own unique style of learning that best fits our lives. However, after speaking with thought leaders, CEOs, and transformation pioneers, a few common core elements emerge to help people do this effectively. The asset below shows the key core dimensions that many of them use to help strengthen and build more sustainable forward-looking skills and continuous, agile learning.

ASSET 3.1: SKILLS AND CONTINUOUS LEARNING - KEY DIMENSIONS

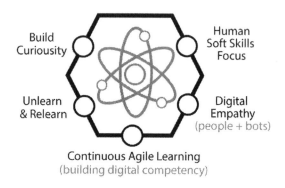

HUMAN SOFT SKILLS FOCUS: As the world becomes more digital, we should focus on becoming more human. As bots start doing the mundane, repetitive tasks, freeing up people, humans can focus more on value creation or soft skills areas. By that, I mean building and strengthening those qualities that are uniquely human, such as communication, creative problem solving, empathy, relationship building, design, and blue-sky thinking. Strengthening these soft skills, whilst repetitive mundane tasks are gradually removed by bots, will not only build your own capabilities with the rise of the machines, but will also provide more sustainable learning habits that you can use in the coming decades.

DIGITAL EMPATHY: In today's digital world, a diverse and disparate group of people and bots are working within businesses – Baby Boomers, Gen Xs, Gen Ys, Gen Zs, with Gen Alphas on the way. Each has their own very unique learning style with various levels of comfort and understanding of digital and mobile technology. Add to this mix the global COVID-19 impacts, cognitive bots, and robots and you have a highly complex web to work with. Understanding how this workforce works best together, listening to your teams, and building trusted relationships will be important skills to develop. To ensure people and teams stay engaged, they need to develop trust in both your leadership and your strategy, and know that there are opportunities for them. It's important that people know that, in a digital world, people are valued and come first. One way to do this is to back and reskill your teams, rather than replace them with bots to reduce headcount and solve a margin issue.

At the 2020 World Economic Forum, the future of work was one of the major topics for debate. It was noted that by 2025, 52% of all labour, as a share of hours spent, will be automated, which is in stark contrast to where we are today. Each generation will have a different approach, skillset, behaviours, and learning styles. This means that if you're managing teams, you'll need a wide and fluid approach to developing agile learning. However, for the sake of simplicity, we can look at the generation spectrum broadly as categorised into two areas: the older generations and the younger ones.

Older generations: Firstly, I apologise in advance for the use of the word "older", but we know that age really is measured by how we feel on the inside, right? As a rule of thumb, board members, mentors, CEOs, executives, senior managers, heads of departments, and senior executives are typically Baby Boomers and Gen Xs. However, it's worth noting that there are waves of CEOs, founders, and executives that are younger Gen Ys and even Gen Zs. Baby Boomers will be between 58 and 74 years old by 2022 and Gen Xs between 47 and 57 years of age. So, to address building Digital EQ for Baby Boomers and Gen Xs means, to some degree, unlearning what you've learned and re-learning new technologies, platforms, and ways of thinking.

Younger generations: The younger, more digitally native generations are sometimes described as Millennials (or Gen Ys), who will be 27–41 years old in 2022; Gen Z, who will be 13–26 years old in 2022; and the Gen Alphas, who will be up to 12 years old in 2022, still at school. The key will be to find a way to influence and drive effective collaboration and partnerships between all the GENs as they start to mingle more in businesses, where mentors and inspiring leaders can impart experience and knowledge, or the "Longevity Dividend", as one CEO I worked with likes to call it, and digital natives can apply design thinking to help solve problems in a different way. Younger generations can leverage the older generations' experience, knowledge, and certainty, while older generations can learn from and empower the younger, more digitally savvy teams.

The Dean of Business at Durham University shared her view around how a collaborative mix of generations in businesses can be a powerful combination.

> *Younger people are more familiar with a mobile and digital world than many of the people that are teaching them in Universities. But these younger minds may not be as familiar with the technicalities, nuances, or practical business fundamentals as the Baby Boomers or the Gen X's. This is where the new generation and older generation can really collaborate and work together in this new digital age.*
>
> —Susan Hart, Executive Dean of Business Durham University

In addition to looking at different learning styles that are generationally driven, it is also important to appreciate learning styles across different genders and cultural diversity. When I spoke with the Chief Executive of ACCA, her perspective was that it is important to look broadly and to get different perspectives.

> *The diversity and inclusion that you need in a business is about different perspectives, not only gender and race. It's a broader understanding that will be the winning formula. It still comes down to people. However good your machines are, it will be people who can or cannot deliver it.*
>
> —Helen Brand, Chief Executive, ACCA

There is tremendous opportunity when you mix diverse and complementary new groups together – the experience and knowledge of the older generations, the dynamic and digital aptitude of the younger generations, and new technology and bots all working together.

In this new digital era, understanding how you, your teams, your exec, and your board are feeling about new, unfamiliar ways of doing business will be crucial;

particularly post-COVID-19, which has accelerated operational challenges relating to remote working, contractor labour through the gig economy, and the adoption of digital (people and bot) teams. The more skilful you are at discerning the feelings behind others' signals, the more effective you will be. So, when faced with someone who doesn't understand how to work with cloud platforms or a bot, or is worried that it will take over their job, or feels they are not technical or don't have the right level of self-awareness to help them through the transition, digital empathy is an important skill to have. Further, the ability to recognise and manage emotions when you or others are confronted with new, rapidly evolving – and sometimes perplexing – technologies is an important part of building your Digital EQ.

We're all only human after all, with a broad cross section of strengths and weaknesses, and a variety of habits and behaviours. Developing your self-awareness means being aware so you can learn and adapt habits and actions that enable positive change. By developing the right values, biases, and attitudes to approach digital innovation, you can manage your and your team's emotions and behaviours better. For some people, this may mean re-learning how you learn.

> *Having a high level of EQ is important. If you use a mallet to hit a nail hard enough and often enough, the nail goes into the wood eventually. But if you use a smarter approach, getting engagement and buy in, you get the full value across the organisation. Given change needs to be end-to-end; it involves people to achieve sustainable success. To succeed in a digital transformation, you have to have a high level of EQ and digital understanding.*
>
> —Raymond Jack, Executive Director, Finance and Operations, ACCA

CONTINUOUS AGILE LEARNING AND BUILDING DIGITAL COMPETENCY: According to the Economic World Congress, if we need to spend an additional 101 days a year learning, this means adopting a whole new approach to learning. To keep up with all the new technologies like robotic process automation, machine learning, cognitive AI, and operating in the cloud, we will need some level of understanding to be effective. These capabilities and skills will be vital to succeed in the digital world. For some, it will mean adapting to different learning styles than that which we were taught. For others, there may be less change; however, being able to consume bite-sized content on a regular basis will be the new norm. The key is to develop a learning programme that is realistic, fits your lifestyle and learning style, and reflects your learning appetite. Albert Einstein's view of learning was that it is a lifelong process.

> *Intellectual growth should commence at birth and cease only at death.*
>
> —Albert Einstein

There is a plethora of great sources of information at your fingertips – using voice commands or, soon, hand-driven gesture activations on mobile devices, not to mention social networks, groups and webinars to help you understand pretty much anything you'd like to know. It really depends on your preferred style of learning and how digitally savvy you are with social media channels and tools. When I've asked leaders how they self-learn, the answers vary depending on their personal style. Some like using LinkedIn, LinkedIn Learning, podcasts, Twitter, or other social media channels. Others like perusing articles from the World Economic Forum, Harvard Business Review, Deloitte, KPMG, EY, PWC, Boston Consulting Group and McKinsey, to name a few, which include some excellent content on all forms of digital transformation, business model redesign, and other relevant material. Global standards and professional bodies like IFAC, IESBA, ACCA, ICAEW, and CIMA are also developing some excellent resources. There is also a growing number of great learning providers such as Blue Prism, Automation Anywhere and UiPath providing short courses on all types of relevant topics, as well as case studies and presentations. It's a digital world and there is really no getting around using digital platforms, apps, and podcasts to develop your knowledge. So, if you're not using digital learning platforms, it may be time to start. It's a great place to dive in and develop your digital skills.

UNLEARN AND RE-LEARN: As new technologies change rapidly, and new ways of doing things are introduced, many people will need to unlearn and re-learn doing things. In a recent discussion with Philomena Leung, Professor of Accounting and Governance at Macquarie University, she was very much of the view that one way to keep up with rapidly changing technology is being open to unlearning, re-learning, and continuously asking questions.

> *You need to unlearn and re-learn to open your mind and look at*
> *different models. To ask questions and become more curious.*
> —Philomena Leung, Professor of Accounting and Governance,
> Macquarie University

In her view, people often don't know how to go about learning in a different way from what they've been taught. It's not easy changing behaviour and it's important to develop a plan to shift from the old to the new to master a new approach.

The Backwards Bike: It can be quite daunting for people who have spent decades learning and perfecting ways of doing things to be faced with the notion of unlearning and re-learning – to now need to develop different ways of thinking and doing business. A good example to consider is the backwards bike experiment, wherein engineer Destin Sandlin built a special bike that operated in reverse. The challenge he created was that when a rider steered the bike to the right, the bike actually turned left, and vice versa. This is obviously the opposite of the way in which a normal bike functions, and it took Destin himself eight months of continuous trying before he was able to actually ride this "backwards" bike. He did this by unlearning and re-learning how to do it, reprogramming his brain in the process to replace the old bike-riding algorithm with a new one.

Sandlin effectively unlearned what he'd learned, and, after practice and commitment, overrode his fundamental instincts to learn a new way of operating. The revelation was that even though the inventor had the knowledge of how the bike worked and what he needed to do, the overcoming of hardwired behaviours did not come easily. Sandlin later tried to ride a normal bike but struggled, as his brain had adapted to a new pattern. It took him around twenty minutes, however, before it all clicked back into place eventually and he could ride the bike like normal. He realised that while you may understand something at a cognitive level, it doesn't mean your behaviour will necessarily change. Clearly, it takes constant effort to change a behaviour or mindset, as well as dedicating time to practise and master it.

Learning is an iterative process that never stops and any person, team, or business that does not evolve and develop their Digital EQ may well find themselves falling behind the curve. In concurrence, Rick Ellis, the previous CEO of CA ANZ, was very clear that today, you need to re-learn how to transform your business to stay relevant:

> *The vast majority of businesses today have to unlearn what they learned a decade ago. You've got to re-learn how to transform your business to be relevant.*
>
> —Rick Ellis, former CEO, CA ANZ and Chairman of Dexibit

As we've seen with the backwards bike example, building these key dimensions will help you to develop forward-looking skills. These, in turn, will ultimately help you keep relevant and be more sustainable for the future. The age of the continuous is here and it's now about constantly learning about these rapidly evolving technologies and platforms.

BUILD CURIOSITY: Developing a heathy curiosity is a great foundation for building continuous forward-learning skills. Having an inquisitive mind opens up the idea of new possibilities, new ways of thinking, and new ways of behaving. Curious people look at different ways of working or different ways to get something done and are usually interested in the world around them. Albert Einstein was once quoted in *Life* magazine, saying:

> *The important thing is not to stop questioning. Curiosity has its own reason for existence. One cannot help but be in awe when he contemplates the mysteries of eternity, of life, of the marvellous structure of reality. It is enough if one tries merely to comprehend a little of this mystery each day. Never lose a holy curiosity.*
>
> —Albert Einstein

Curious people usually ask lots of questions. Business opportunities can often be found in answering some simple but powerful questions; for example:

CAN I TURN THE CAPITAL COMMITMENT INTO A NEW REVENUE STREAM
WHAT COULD I DO WITH THIS NEW TECHNOLOGY
WHY DOES IT COST SO MUCH
WHY DOES IT TAKE SO LONG   CAN I CUT OUT THE MIDDLE MAN
COULD I APPLY NEW ANALYTICS TO BIG-DATA SETS TO CREATE BETTER CUSTOMER EXPERIENCES

In a multibillion-dollar bank I recently met with, the finance team was genuinely excited when they actually experienced the benefits of their RPA initiative. Not having to be kept from family late at night was a very tangible and valuable benefit that we discussed. Once the team saw things gradually improving, they became more curious and started to come up with their own RPA initiatives, which proved contagious and drove further involvement with the programme.

If you're not naturally curious, then start by getting into the habit of asking more questions. Why do your business processes take so long? Could the process benefit from automation? Another approach is to start with something small and explore a new topic, or an area you've always been interested in but never got around to investigating. It's important to develop a level of curiosity in a world with a whole lot of new technology that many of us need to have at least a fundamental appreciation for, even if you don't need to be a subject matter expert. It's about exercising and building your curiosity muscle to strengthen it. The good news is that mobile smart devices make accessing information infinitely accessible with courses, audio tapes, reports, and whatever format you prefer.

As a rule of thumb, it generally takes a focused thirty-day commitment to change a behaviour. Setting yourself the task of having a month-long plan to ask questions can help spark your curiosity. It stands to reason that if your business is just starting on the transformation curve and you're building stronger digital skills and awareness of things like the latest cloud platforms, cognitive RPA, APIs, centralised data architecture, and agile business models, you can better help drive the business agenda. Start to get curious and build your capability, which in turn builds more trust in this complex new digital era.

By building **curiosity**, establishing a **continuous agile learning** culture and facilitating **unlearning** of the old and **re-learning** of the new, you can stay relevant in today's increasingly digital world. Exercising **digital empathy** to navigate digital dilemmas and taking a **human soft skill focus** to bring out what humans do best and set them apart from machines will help you to build forward-looking skills and put your people first.

In our example in the last chapter, Ali, Global Head of Funds Management, grappled with how to lead a team that feared losing their jobs. They were similarly wary of and not at all used to working with bots, or disruptive design thinking processes that automated fees and billing manual tasks. Firstly, the Head of Funds knew he had to do things differently from how he'd been doing things in the past. He applied the very simple, but effective, WHAT-WHY-HOW model to create a robust plan.

WHAT he needed to do. What was the point of it? What was his strategy? Was the proof of concept robust, showing clear outcomes? What were the results backing up the proof of concept and what was the impact to the strategy and long-term upside? What new partnerships did he need to develop? What was the value to customers, the community, and shareholders? He needed to convince himself and others that what he was doing was valuable.

WHY he recommended this course of action. Why was it the right thing to do? Why should the executive believe his approach was better than the current manual processes? Why should the team believe him and get invested? Why should they care and get behind it? Why should the business do this? Often, if there is resistance to change, or unlearning and re-learning is involved, this can present challenges. So, having a clear and compelling WHY helps give you the conviction and reason to persist in the face of challenge.

HOW he was going to implement and sustain the project. How was he going to drive change and get from here to there? How would the programme deliver to the business strategy? How was he going to get different teams from different departments with different learning styles and perspectives working together and collaborating? How was he going to disrupt the BAU way of thinking and infuse a fresh approach?

Ali had to adopt new behaviours to build forward-learning skills. By continuously asking questions and stimulating **curiosity,** he motivated his team, building their interest and involvement through the transformation. Ali applied **digital empathy** by spending considerable time helping his team really understand what was in it for them and going through the change process. He was acutely aware that his team was not convinced about the benefit of an automation programme, and some had anxiety around potentially losing their jobs. Ali demonstrated that he genuinely cared about their personal success as they faced new digital challenges by setting a clear direction, backed up with a solid business case and impressive proof of concept. Introducing university students into the design process was a good way to help his team **unlearn and re-learn** a better way forward with an automated process.

By assessing his team's digital capabilities and skills required to deliver the programme, Ali redeveloped their job descriptions to remove repetitive automatable tasks and free up his team for value creation work. By driving design thinking and partner-building skills within the various teams made up of engineers, accountants, and technology, Ali was able to develop a more **human soft skill focus** and build those soft human skills using a digital lens. In doing so, other divisions were able to learn from each other; some were even upskilled to become subject matter experts within the business to help other divisions learn and adapt. He set up a Centre of Excellence (CoE) to drive **continuous agile learning**, where the business could constantly reflect and learn from the successes and failures of similar projects and advancements.

So, to sum up, put people first and develop their continuous learning skills. Focus on building definitive human behaviours and soft skills for yourself and your teams as bots start to take up the more repetitive and mundane tasks. Build digital empathy to better help people through digital transformations or evolutions where needed and unlearn less effective habits and re-learn more effective new ones. Finally, find ways to build curiosity and develop genuine excitement about change, rather than fear or resistance.

EXERCISE 3 – SKILLS AND CONTINUOUS LEARNING - SELF ASSESSMENT

Business and finance professionals need to stay abreast of new technologies, platforms, and conversations to stay relevant and be effective. Go to www.taketherobotoutofthehuman.com/exercises, and use SHAPE1 as the password to fill in the skills and continuous-learning self-assessment that poses questions designed to start you thinking about your own learning approach, as well as areas to consider for development as you build your Digital EQ.

CASE STUDY – MULTIBILLION-DOLLAR GLOBAL INSURANCE COMPANY

THE CHALLENGE: A leading multibillion-dollar global insurance company, over 100 years old with over 50,000 employees, was well on the path and progressing along their digital transformation journey. However, as is the case for most businesses today, they needed to do more with less. They endeavoured to find efficiencies and cost reductions, while still providing exemplary customer service as their business digitally evolved. Ideally, the intention was to do this without losing good people and to continue to improve customer outcomes and build curiosity across the business. However, while some areas of the business were well advanced in automation, many of their employees didn't have the exposure, confidence or understanding to effectively grow alongside the necessary digital transformation.

THE SOLUTION: In addition to the internal HR and personal development plans, they developed several simple but effective initiatives to help continually develop curiosity, open people's eyes to new technology, and provide a better understanding of the value of automation and its benefits. The four improvement initiatives implemented were:

RIDE THE RAILWAY – To address a basic fear and lack of automation and digital transformation, they developed a programme called Ride the Railway, wherein employees spend a day rotating around different departments. The only cost is time, with a one-day rotation to spend in different teams.

BUILD A BOT IN A DAY – The company put a programme in place to address automation principles called the "bot-in-a-day programme." After choosing an area in the business that has no exposure to automation or RPA and where the teams don't really know what it's all about, the change team find a business problem they can solve in a day. SMEs from their continuous improvements team then work with the team to consider the problem and deliver the solution in a day. The team witnessed first-hand that you don't need to know how to code to build a bot. They were able to further see that while it doesn't take much time or money to deliver, you can achieve results in a single day that eliminate mundane, repetitive tasks and make people's lives easier in the long run.

OPEN DAYS – The company also holds open days with a show-and-tell approach to automation successes and sends improvement teams into department social meetings, or whatever group activity makes sense, to show them tangible results.

OPERATIONALISED WORKSHOPS – These are dedicated workshops with different teams and departments, designed to encourage teams that may not be overly familiar with automation and work through real-time problem-solutions and the benefits automation can bring. They further drive engagement by allocating specific processes to managers who take responsibility for the delivery of that process.

THE RESULTS: Improved understanding of the value of automation. Building curiosity and readiness to scale. Hundreds of people internally have gone through the Ride the Railway programme, subsequently gaining exposure to other divisions and technologies and seeing the value to them. These initiatives contribute to a vast majority of new hires being internal candidates, with very low staff attrition rates overall.

CHAPTER 4

HUMAN (CUSTOMER) FOCUS

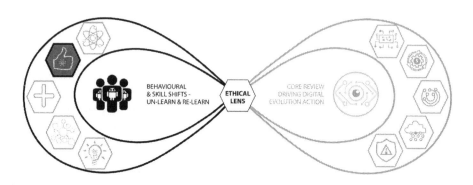

Regardless of what industry you're in, customers expect their dealings with your business to be better, faster, easier, intuitive and tailored to their needs. With many high-performing, tech-savvy businesses like Uber, Airbnb, Tesla, and Netflix setting the pace for rising customer expectations, people today want more seamless and richer experiences. This means it's important to build human interactions and develop a customer-centric focus across your business to meet and connect the rapidly evolving digital and mobile habits of customers today.

As you begin to implement AI-driven solutions, it's also important that you have humans in the loop to ensure biases don't creep into algorithmic processes, ethical frameworks are expanded to account for cognitive automation scenarios, processes are redesigned to be more sustainable and suited to humans and algorithms working together, and value-based quality controls are in place as things become less physical and more digital. With the rapid adoption of AI automating complex business processes, ensuring humans are in the loop will be essential.

I recently met with a global insurance business valued at around $400 billion. With a customer-centric focus driven through their business strategy, they have successfully implemented over fifty RPA bots across the UK, North America, Germany, and Switzerland, streamlining over a hundred processes, as well as 1.3 million transactions across claims, underwriting, and finance. They're trialling innovative technology platforms to enable unstructured data and AI-based claims management using platforms like ABBYY, Flexi, and Cognito. Off the back of this, they are yielding some great results, like reducing times to present claims to underwriters from six days to two hours, as well as introducing AI-driven mobile app-based life insurance predictors to help customers choose the best plans. These outcomes were achieved as a result of having a clear, customer-centric focus to help underpin their digital transformation journey. In addition, these initiatives were developed with humans intrinsic and woven into the process.

Right now, businesses are working hard to stay relevant in the eyes of their customers and provide great customer experiences in a world that is diving headfirst into the digital depths of AI. However, the challenge many businesses face today is that building an effective customer-centric focus, if it doesn't already exist, can be a daunting task. It also means that you may need to unlearn and re-learn some well-established old habits, approaches, and behaviours to build a meaningful customer-focus culture and make it stick.

The good news is that building strong foundations for customer focus and building humans into the loop across processes and AI initiatives can be achieved, regardless of where your business is on its digital transformational journey, by following some basic principles. In this chapter, we'll look at these to help you:

- build stronger customer relevance
- ensure humans are in the loop with AI-fuelled initiatives
- understand the importance of walking in the customer's shoes
- adopt a one-team mentality to help break down silos

- understand the need to develop effective measurement across the entire customer journey to drive insights, improvements and business value
- realise the importance of agile customer feedback
- understand centralised data and the need for agile, driven insights and ecosystems

We'll then look at why this is important, and, finally, we'll explore how you can build this more robust human (customer-centric) focus.

SO, WHAT IS A HUMAN (CUSTOMER) FOCUS?

What does a customer focus really mean? Simply put, it means placing the customer at the centre of your business to help meet their needs and to get all the customer touch points working together to provide the best possible product or service to grow your business – as well as ensuring there is a balanced AI and human relationship where 'humans are in the loop'. Now, in a digital world, people rely heavily on their mobile smart devices. They want instant information via a wide variety of channels like social media, and expect fast easy transactions online. This means that your customer touch points, and delivery platforms, need to be far more connected, automated to some extent, and ideally AI-fuelled to be effective. So, it's important to embrace the notion that customer touch points are vastly different today than they were a decade ago and to consider how your business model can best evolve in this digital world.

Savvy business leaders recognise the power of having a customer focus that, when mixed with innovation and new technology, helps to meet the changing needs of customers. In a recent media release, Zurich's Group CEO Mario Greco outlined his commitment to customer focus:

> We have deepened our customer focus and employee engagement by listening to their needs through regular tailored surveys. We have empowered employees to drive change and given our younger generation a stronger voice in shaping our culture and innovative programmes such as our Zurich Innovation Championship for

startups. We will build on our achievements to further transform insurance, using technology to meet changing needs and create rewarding experiences.

—Group CEO Mario Greco, Zurich

The Group CEO of Zurich recognised the vital importance of developing a holistic, customer-centric focus to help power his multibillion-dollar business.

The customer journey starts from the first moment a potential customer engages with your business – from the perception you create of your organisation, how you demonstrate your social conscience, what your business is doing for the community (and the planet), what partners you have and what their values are, as well as how valuable and useful your products and services are to them. The first customer contact often begins through word of mouth from friends, the media, social media, your website, or physical stores and ideally should continue well after they've received your product or service. Customers also consider how easy you are to do business with using mobile, digital, and physical touch points – and this includes service and interactions after they have bought from you. In fact, customers are assessing your business at every touch point across their experience with your business and forming a view as to whether they want to proceed or not. So, it's important that you focus on the entire customer experience to work out how you can improve.

Apple, a brand that needs no introduction, is known for its relentless focus on delivering exceptional customer experiences. The first Apple store opened on May 19, 2001 in Virginia, USA with a share price of $1.68. Today, Apple is one of the most valuable companies in the world. Apple implemented a long-term, customer-first strategy to build genuine relationships with their customers. Apple ensures that every customer touchpoint – including their app store, website, social media, retail stores, staff engagement, and, of course, their smart products – delivers a consistently high "A.P.P.L.E." experience, which is a five-step customer service approach.

A – approach customers with a personalised and warm welcome

P – probe politely to understand the customer's needs

P – present a solution for the customer to take home

L – listen for and resolve issues or concerns

E – end with a fond farewell and invitation to return

A customer focus takes on many shapes and sizes depending on what business you're in and what your strategy looks like. So, if one of your business goals is to have more customers to be successful and to achieve your company ambitions, then having a customer focus is a great place to begin.

WHY HAVE A HUMAN (CUSTOMER) FOCUS?

Having a customer focus helps your business stay relevant, improves your ability to build potential customers, and helps set a roadmap for your digital evolution. According to McKinsey, customer experience is an excellent starting point for a digital transformation, but it also helps to deliver material business results, with around 30% uplifts in customer satisfaction, 20% improvements in employee satisfaction, and up to 50% uplifts in economic gains.

When I spoke with the General Manager of Innovations at CA ANZ, he shared a similar view where the customer must be central to any business model transformation.

> When you think business model transformation, it should be on behalf of the customer. That's why client satisfaction is so important. It's not 'what solutions I offer,' but 'what problems I solve.' Many businesses are still focused on 'what I offer.'
>
> —Sunny Sirabas, GM Innovation, CA ANZ

By understanding what's important to your customers and why they value these things, you can provide the focus to evolve your business model to provide them with what they want, when they want, in the way they want.

Apple's success is greatly attributed to not only product innovation attracting millions of customers, but having a relentless, ongoing commitment to customer service that greatly contributes to their trillion-dollar worth. A customer-centric focus is an essential part of any successful business and in today's fast-paced digital world, it's even more important to deliver better customer satisfaction and better employee engagement, and yield uplifted economic gains.

HOW CAN I DEVELOP A HUMAN (CUSTOMER) FOCUS?

A human (customer) focus should be ingrained within your business blueprint. Ideally it starts as a core strategic pillar where the customer satisfaction is at the heart of your business model and strategy. If it's not already ingrained, depending on your business's digital maturity, developing a customer focus may require a mindset shift – to unlearn the old ways of managing customers and re-learn a more effective approach that puts them at the centre of everything you do as a business in a digital world. This includes breaking down any siloed thinking or behaviour and adopting a one-team approach. It also means building a proactive customer-focused culture right across the business with common goals and a continuous improvement philosophy. Once you've hardwired a customer-centric focus into your business strategy, you need tools to enable your teams to improve the customer experience, such as centralised, connected data with analytics that drive insights supported by the right technology platforms – a single-view, holistic measurement of the customer journey with an agile customer feedback loop where you can take customer feedback and feed it directly into your business to improve processes, systems, or experiences. The level of sophistication of these activities will depend on your business's digital maturity and strategy; however, regardless of how sophisticated or agile your business model currently is, these principles can be used whether you're just starting on the digital journey, getting your stride, or really moving and digitally advanced.

As to humans in the loop with AI-driven initiatives, it is about ensuring that any automated process, workflow and decision points have human interventions built into them. This enables you to not only reduce risk, protect public interest, maintain a sound degree of compliance and efficiency, but to enhance the outcomes through leveraging the best of both worlds: human creativity combined with automated and efficient AI.

So, regardless of where you sit on the digital transformation curve, the six principles in the asset below illustrate the key customer focus dimensions that can help you develop a human (customer) focus within your own business.

ASSET 4.1: HUMAN (CUSTOMER) FOCUS DIMENSIONS

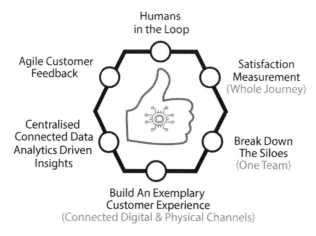

Whether your business is AI-fuelled with a cloud-based, single-source data lake and highly automated analytics, or it's manually process-based and macro spreadsheet-driven, the following principles apply.

HUMANS IN THE LOOP: The combination of both humans and AI is far more powerful than either one on its own, at this point in time. If automation or AI is built to enhance and help humans, then building systems around human interaction delivers an end result that better harnesses human judgement, creativity, ethics and oversight. It's about finding the right balance between AI and human interactions and processes that will deliver sustainable results, and this will be driven to some degree by how advanced your business's digital maturity is. Even if you're still on the starting line on the digital evolution curve, you can still look at automating and improving manual processes that are more sustainable to set the stage for when your business is ready to start its evolution.

JOURNEY SATISFACTION MEASUREMENT: Most businesses measure customer satisfaction in some way or another. However, many may struggle to connect measurement with deriving real value for the customer and creating long-term value for the business. Either the measurement isn't robust, or it's only partially useful, or you're simply measuring the wrong things. In addition, as many businesses are still siloed in nature, the strategies are often not fully aligned, with solutions perhaps only looking at sections of the customer journey rather than the total experience. It's important to work collaboratively across the business, develop an overarching KPI like an NPS score, then unpack this and identify across each business unit what elements make up the overall customer experience and measure them.

A good place to start is in the customers' shoes. Understand who they are, what they want, what's important to them and what value looks like to them. Work out what experience you want your customers to have and then work backwards. Map this against your business's capability and then, depending on how digitally mature your business is, start prioritising and addressing the weak links across the customer experience journey map – whether it's brand-related with online research, via social media review, store-related through the physical customer experience, purchasing online to see how easy the experience is, or fulfilment of the product from the warehouse to the courier to the customer. The whole journey touches multiple areas of the business, but these need to be viewed as a one-customer journey. Develop an understanding of the total customer journey experience, and, depending on your business's digital awareness and capability, find ways to deliver the best possible service or product that you can.

BREAKING DOWN THE SILOES – ONE TEAM: Regardless of your current business structure or digital maturity, working towards breaking down barriers and silo-busting is a good way to start to drive a more holistic customer view and deliver a better customer experience. Many businesses are made up of multiple divisions in more typical, siloed company structures where the goals and KPIs are often vertically clear, but not always horizontally integrated across the business for key strategic programmes. This is further fuelled by each division having its own specific objectives and outcomes that may not be aligned. Approaching customer service horizontally across the business will help develop a common goal and more of a focus for the business. This will, in turn, help rally the teams to start to look at solutions that matter most along the whole of the customer journey – by having a customer service focus that is embedded within the bones of your business and will help drive the right culture and business outcomes.

BUILD AN EXEMPLARY CUSTOMER EXPERIENCE: If your goal is to deliver the best customer experience possible, delivering the right products and service, you need to look at connecting digital and physical experiences with your business. It is also important to understand what role your technology platforms currently play and, more importantly, what is required to enable an exemplary customer experience. It means working with operations, marketing, legal, sales, technology, product, finance, transformation teams, and customers to understand and identify the right tools to drive the business sustainably.

Look at what problems you solve for your customer as opposed to what products you offer. Have a look at your business's social media presence. Go onto your own website and search for the product or service you're trying to buy. Then try to buy it. Was the process seamless, enjoyable, and exemplary? Phone your call centre or engage with your chatbots to get a feeling for what your customers are experiencing when they engage with your business. Is it a simple process or are there delays, glitches, and lags? Did you receive any follow-up communication when you enquired? What was it like? Start to build a clear picture of how good the customer journey experience is and where there is room to improve. Then, look at what customer feedback you currently have available. How is this information being actioned? What measures do you have in place? Do you have the right culture to drive a great customer experience?

It's important that the customer experience is viewed across the business and not in disconnected siloes. When I spoke with the head of transformation at a leading insurance business, he shared a similar view:

> *End-to-end automation is an interconnected piece of lots of different things, as long as the customer experience is seamless. How you do that in the background doesn't really matter as long as it's fast, accurate, timely, and easy for the customer.*
>
> —Alastair Robertson, Head of Continuous Improvement & Automation,
> Zurich UK

However, given customers today are more mobile and digitally savvy than ever before, this also involves having the right business model, data strategy, and digital skills to meet the ever-rising needs of your customers. It also means ensuring your business carefully considers the right technology to drive improved customer experiences.

McDonalds' recent advancements in the technology space are transforming their customers' experiences in and around their restaurants. Providing customers with more ways to personalise their orders is, in turn, meeting their needs. In March 2019, McDonalds made two acquisitions to help strengthen their customer experience. The first was Dynamic Yield, a machine learning leader in personalisation and decision logic technology to help with customisation. The second was Apptrente, a voice AI system focused on fast-food ordering to enable customer personalisation. Dynamic Yield's technology allowed McDonalds to change the drive-thru menu based on the weather, time of day, current restaurant traffic, and trending menus, leaving upselling to the new technology so the staff can focus on the customer service. Steve Easterbrook, President and CEO of the McDonalds Corporation, recently talked about this shift to a more customer-centric focus:

> *Technology is a critical element of our Velocity Growth Plan, enhancing the experience for our customers by providing greater convenience on their terms.... With this acquisition, we're expanding both our ability to increase the role technology and data will play in our future and the speed with which we'll be able to implement our vision of creating more personalised experiences for our customers.*
> —Steve Easterbrook, President and CEO, McDonalds Corporation

The reality is that some businesses today are not in a position to make this slow, balanced kind of type of business change, where their digital transformation journey may happen slowly over time to balance risk and reward. Processes and systems that are complex and less agile can be a huge frustration to everyone, so finding ways to innovate low-hanging fruit aspects of customer experience is a good place to start. These areas are typically those that would greatly be improved from automation, with large gains and minimal business disruption.

So, sometimes it's about working within the confines of your current business model and finding ways in the short term to deliver better customer service regardless of where you are along your digital transformation curve. Sometimes this requires thinking out of the box and applying blue-sky thinking.

> *Blue-sky thinking would be to build from the ideal customer experience and work back. However, because we're a hundred-year-old company with various legacy systems, we could easily get caught up focusing all our time trying to fix the internal stuff. Right now, it's about how we can have direct impact on delivering a better customer experience – speeding up claims, keeping customers updated, prioritising complaints, and looking at customer feedback to quickly respond.*
>
> —Alastair Robertson, Head of Continuous Improvement & Automation,
>
> Zurich UK

CENTRALISED, CONNECTED, DATA ANALYTICS-DRIVEN INSIGHTS: Having one source of data, a "single source of truth" with a holistic customer view, is the shining star that many businesses are striving to achieve. It's also a race to get there before your competition so you can build better customer experiences and offerings from insights derived from the data and analytics. With a central view across the customer journeys, it means your business can be far nimbler, timelier, and more effective with your customer interactions. One UK-based Aerospace and Defence business I'm currently working with has just rebuilt its data architecture, moving towards a data lake model with central data repository (CDR). While this will happen in stages, they have recognised the significance of having a CDR and are building a strategy to unlock their customer insights.

Many businesses have customer improvement aspirations that are at odds with their current operations, business models, systems, structures, or data capabilities. Often these revolve around having a clear data strategy with a centralised, cloud-based data lake or repository where all the business platforms can interconnect without confusing or compromising the data flows and analytics. The challenge is that many businesses have extensive legacy systems that often were acquired with considerable capital expenditure.

So, new platforms to sustain the long term need to be considered, which may include scrapping the old and starting fresh with the new.

While developing the best-in-class data strategy may be phased over five years, the important thing is to get on the journey and start to move towards an environment that allows you to effectively analyse customer data to improve their experience. Working towards this will help reveal and unlock valuable insights that up until now may have been buried in the data.

AGILE CUSTOMER FEEDBACK: It's imperative to have an agile customer feedback loop. This means getting information in a timely fashion and having an agile reporting setup so that you can act on that information quickly. You must ensure that the feedback is widely accessible by all teams to provide greater transparency on the customer journey, rather than merely focusing on one isolated aspect; for example, time spent on a website to transact and buy a product. If someone spends a long time on your ecommerce "buy now" page, it may be construed as a great result. However, often, it's a case of the website page being difficult to navigate, meaning it takes people a long time to search for what they want. If you look more broadly at what customers are doing next, you may see that 80% drop off. If all you do is look at the time on the ecommerce page, it fails to give the right information. Instead, looking at the whole customer journey paints a clearer picture and better highlights areas to focus on. Then, take that information and use it to adjust a process, answer a query, or respond to a complaint as efficiently as possible so that the business is in tune with its customers.

These six core principles above apply regardless of where your business is on the digital transformation path. In the insurance business example at the beginning of this chapter, they improved customer experience by developing a one-team approach rather than just working in siloes, as well as really understanding their customers and standing in their shoes. They used agile customer feedback loops to look closely at what customers were saying in regular leadership team meetings and responding within twenty-four hours. They used transactional net promoter scores to assess satisfaction measures to see how they could improve the whole of the customer journey, and they used this data, although not centralised, to help drive decisions. All of these elements, when combined, helped to drive an improved customer experience.

Finally, a customer-centric focus should be a core part of your business strategy. Once you have identified your ideal customer journey and the metrics to drive change, this should be hardwired across every department through connected, integrated goals. This way, the whole business is working together with focus, driving towards a common end result. As an analogy, it's a little like a rocket taking off from earth. If all the thrusters are focused and pointed in one direction, the rocket can break free of the earth's gravitational pull. However, if a few of these thrusters are pointing in opposing directions, then the rocket will spin out of control and likely crash and burn. Getting the whole business behind an idea and getting them to all work together to deliver it is the key.

EXERCISE 4 – HUMAN (CUSTOMER) FOCUS – WHERE ARE YOU AT?

To assess your strengths, visit www.taketherobotoutofthehuman.com/exercises to identify how developed your human (customer) focus is. In a world of heightened digital customer experience—fueled by AI and big data insights—it will be important to have a strong customer lens, coupled with the discipline to ensure humans are in the loop when building cognitive automated initiatives.

CASE STUDY – THE RISE OF NETFLIX THROUGH DIGITAL EVOLUTION

Some of you may remember Blockbuster Video, an American-based company that offered home movie and video game rental services through over nine thousand stores around the world. It became a global business in the 1990s, but later lost its relevance and suffered at the hands of competition from Netflix and other video-on-demand services. Blockbuster turned down a sale offer from Netflix for $50 million in 2000, later filing for bankruptcy in 2010 after declining sales continued.

Netflix, now worth in the hundreds of billions of dollars and with over two hundred million subscribers, began as a small startup online DVD rental service, and through digitally transforming its business to meet growing customer needs, it has changed the way people watch movies through its online streaming service. At the core of Netflix's business model was the customer value proposition, whereas the Blockbuster customer experience was far from ideal as technology improved. I recall visiting Blockbuster and spending more time than I'd rather sifting through possible movie choices only to find that the movies you wanted were either out being rented or incurred a premium charge. Then, after you'd watched the movie, you generally couldn't quite find a way to drop them back to the store in the twenty-four-hour window and were charged a late fee. It was like borrowing a book from a library. Store visits were time-consuming, there were no effective catalogues, and you needed to own a video cassette recorder (VCR machine), and later a Digital Versatile Disc (DVD) player, to play the movie.

Netflix capitalised on the gap in the market and built an innovative business model that met consumer needs and made it easy to watch movies. As an online service, Netflix enabled its customers to choose movies from a digital catalogue from any device to either own or rent then play instantly, with a monthly subscription service for unlimited rentals. In 2013, Netflix went on to develop its own content, like *House of Cards*, using the high volumes of customer data they had analysed to identify what actors, genres, titles, sequels, and plots seemed to work the best for specific demographics. Netflix embraced the customers' desires to personalise by developing a smart content recommendation system using machine learning and big data analytics to serve up tailored content to suit the user. Netflix's popularity grew and the rest is history.

Of course, even with more mature digital businesses, innovation doesn't stop. Netflix has been extending the customer experience to team up with mobile carriers – Amazon, Google Home, and others – to keep the product and service relevant and ahead of the curve. Fuelling the innovation is a unique entrepreneurial culture that goes hand in hand with a nimbler, agile, data insight-centric business, where their core philosophy is that of people over process. So, they have great people working together with what Netflix describes as real values of **judgement**, **communication**, **curiosity**, **courage**, **passion**, **selflessness**, **innovation**, **inclusion**, **integrity**, and **impact**. They encourage independent decision making by employees, and share information openly, broadly, and deliberately.

CHAPTER 5

AMPLIFIED VALUE CREATION MINDSET

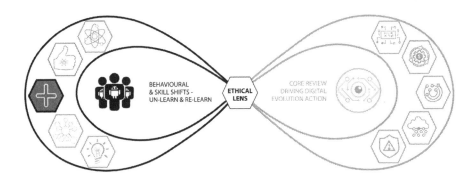

At the 2020 Oracle OpenWorld in London, an inspiring session outlined a world first initiative called the World Bee Project. Using AI, IoT, blockchain, cloud-based big data and analytics, wireless technologies and robotics, its members endeavoured to find solutions to the alarming drop in bee population globally. Now, you might ask, what's the big deal with bees?

The real-world problem is that bees don't just sting and produce honey; they are also one of the most crucial links in our food chain as pollinators. Since the late 1990s, the world's bee population has been driven towards extinction by diverse pressures, many of them man-made. Bees are a keystone species, and are vital to the agricultural industry, with 1.4 billion farming jobs and 75% of the world's food supply dependent on the pollination of crops. The UN Food and Agriculture Organisation stated that there are a hundred crop species that provide 90% of food around the world, and more than seventy of these species are pollinated by bees. Without bees, it's estimated that there would be half the amount of fruit and vegetables in our supermarkets.

Bees pollinate the trees that create the oxygen we breathe, contributing to the balance of our global climate. Bees improve the yield of commercially produced crops and act as natural agents of pollination. There have even been experiments with artificial pollination and robot bees; however, the artificial alternative is unable to provide the same level of nutrition in food products as natural bee pollination. So, it's hard to beat mother nature.

The Executive President and Founder of the World Bee Project, Sabiha Malik, applied blue-sky thinking with a big, audacious goal that has global impact. She described the initiative as:

> *...including the use of AI, IoT, data analytics, computer vision, wireless technologies, and robotics in advanced ways to discover new insights and create new solutions to serve bees and pollinators, food production, livelihoods, wildlife conservation, and to mitigate the climate emergency. In fact, to ensure our survival on earth.*
>
> —Sabiha Malik, Executive President and
> Founder of the World Bee Project

By utilising cloud storage and AI analytics, they gained insights through data to improve pollinators' habitats, create more sustainable ecosystems, and improve food security and nutrition. The Global Hive Network is now the world's first globally coordinated honeybee hive monitoring initiative designed to generate unprecedented new data, creating meaningful correlations about honeybee health as a result.

Businesses today are looking for ways to differentiate from the competitive clutter and find a sustainable edge. However, the challenge many businesses face is that adopting and applying a value creation mindset is a vastly different way of thinking and, with new technology exploding into the market, requires a mindset reset. As humans, we are creatures of habit and tend to solve problems the way we were brought up or taught. The difference now is that with the flood of AI-fuelled businesses, new technology, and far more complex ecosystems available, the game has changed. This means thinking outside the box to help develop more innovative business solutions, where you may need to unlearn and re-learn ways of approaching problems to think more broadly and differently to build greater value in this new digital age.

The good news is you can start to shift your thinking and build more innovation by following some basic principles that many of the thought leaders and pioneers use. In this chapter, we'll look at:

- building a stronger amplified value creation mindset
- the importance of unshackling through automation to free up your time
- using creative problem solving and blue-sky thinking
- focusing on outcomes that have a sustainable value focus
- delivery across community, social, environmental, as well as profit
- business financial and product value

We'll then look at why this is important, and, finally, we'll explore how you can build this more robust value creation mindset.

WHAT IS AN AMPLIFIED VALUE CREATION MINDSET?

Amplified value creation means creating exponential value for a broad spectrum of stakeholders including shareholders, owners, customers, employees, the community, and even the very planet we live on. As an indicator, a cursory glance at the topics covered by the World Economic Forum provides good insight into some of these areas of interest, such as sustainability, global warming, the future of cities, business models, and digital transformation, and the future of work and AI in the fourth industrial revolution. In the World Bee Project example above, the social, community, and environmental gains are fairly self-evident, and the project clearly delivers value across a broad spectrum of stakeholders.

For businesses, value creation is often more about long-term shareholder value to ensure you have a sustainable and relevant business model. This means ensuring your business priorities are sound but extending beyond shorter-term profits and embracing strong social, environmental, employee, and community outcomes. Value creation is about igniting or creating ideas, and developing ecosystem partnerships and solutions to overcome complex problems and derive real value across broader groups.

An amplified value creation mindset is a different way of thinking about problems, solutions, and possibilities that deliver broader value. This can now be better realised as automation helps to unshackle our minds from manual tasks that are better suited to robots or algorithms, allowing us to do more out-of-the-box creative thinking around business challenges and solutions – not just in one-off annual strategy workshops, but as part of an ongoing, more fluid business process.

The balance, of course, revolves around ensuring that the value creation solution benefits broad stakeholder groups, but at the same time, being realistic about delivering products and services that are valuable, profitable, and sustain the company's future. It's about ensuring that you have core products and services that can be delivered effectively once their manufacturing, development, and/or distribution is automated. With more time for creative thinking, you are free from your proverbial manual shackles, free now to explore how better to utilise new technologies and capabilities like big data, IoT, and cognitive smart automation that better enables possibilities that you previously did not have the time, bandwidth, or tools to create.

HOW CAN I DEVELOP AN AMPLIFIED VALUE CREATION MINDSET?

As we've discussed in previous chapters, it takes time and effort to change any well-established behaviour or habit. Building a value creation mindset is no different. The easier part is rewiring an old process to a new, more sustainable one. The more challenging part is shifting your behaviour, particularly across your whole business, and, like many today, you may hit roadblocks because of digital awareness or levels of understanding based on your business's digital maturity.

If your operating model is not sufficiently agile or digitally enabled, the question is where to start. How can you effectively start thinking in a way unshackled by automation? Basically, you need to put a digital-transformation-change-agent hat on to help drive the right level of business change. The asset below outlines the core principles that will help you shift to a more value creation mindset.

ASSET 5.1: AMPLIFIED VALUE CREATION MINDSET

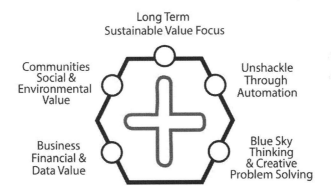

LONG-TERM SUSTAINABLE VALUE FOCUS: Today, businesses must deliver financial value with improved social and environmental benefits. People are holding businesses to account, to deliver a higher standard of responsible values and more effective environmental, social, and corporate governance (ESG). If your business does not embrace these sustainability values within its DNA across management, systems, processes, and culture it will be at real risk of losing relevance, appeal, and customers in the long term.

A recent Accenture report on shaping sustainable organisations highlighted that 74% of consumers believe that ethical corporate practices and values are an important reason to choose a brand. Further, that companies with a stronger strong sustainability DNA are more likely to deliver financial value and positive impact on society and the environment. The report went on to say that EBITDA margins of top quartile companies index 21% higher compared to bottom quartile and that their sustainability performance is around 21% higher. The real opportunity is not just adding efficiency measures and reporting, but in rethinking and rede-signing your business model to amplify innovation and deliver real value.

UNSHACKLE THROUGH AUTOMATION: As your business begins to auto-mate and implement cognitive and algorithms, you, your team, and your busi-ness will be freed up to do more value-creation thinking. You can explore the initiatives you've always wanted to but didn't have the time or capacity to. It is imperative to move away from being bogged down with a continual, manual-fix mindset and allow the bots to take over the repetitive workload to free up your mind.

In the World Bee Project example, they were able to bring the idea to life by unshackling from labour-intensive, manual, unconnected processes through a combination of AI, IoT, wireless technologies, and advanced robotics to drive a more automated, sustainable success where the end results are tremendous value created for communities and the environment. This initiative became a reality by applying value-creation thinking. By combining data from sensors in the Global Hive Network and world-leading bee research with AI, they were able to gener-ate and access new insights that can help inform and implement global actions to improve pollinator habitats, create more sustainable ecosystems, and improve food security, nutrition, and livelihoods.

COMMUNITIES, SOCIAL, AND ENVIRONMENTAL VALUE: From a busi-ness perspective, priorities in the past have long been revenue-based or centred around shareholder return as the number one focus. Customer satisfaction, community involvement, and environmentally friendly impacts have tradition-ally been stationed down the priority line. Now, the priorities are shifting. At the World Economic Forum in Davos, it was outlined that social, community, and sustainability-based focuses are starting to play a larger role. Shareholder return, while still vital to keep businesses viable, is shifting in priority. With the global warming crisis building, developing products and services that deliver something tangible and material back to communities and the environment is becoming more relevant and important. Low-carbon emissions, low plastics, environmentally and community friendly are quickly becoming the norm. Social responsibility and environmental accountability are becoming expected by-products of any product and service; and with the world heading towards a global warming crisis, coupled with Gen Y, Z, and Alpha's sentiments around protecting our world front and centre, ensuring your product and service stack up will be very important in the coming years.

DuPont, a well-known manufacturer of the plastic material Teflon, in West Virginia, USA, is a good example of shareholder returns in the past being the focus at the expense of communities and the environment. It was implied that they had knowledge that their plants and product were toxic to the environment and to people around the world. Yet, despite this, the business still kept manufacturing their products. In February 2017, DuPont settled over 3,550 PFOA lawsuits for $671 million, but denied any wrongdoing.

Tony's Chocolonely is a Dutch chocolate manufacturer which not only creates great-tasting chocolate with flavours like "dark milk pretzel toffee" and "milk caramel sea salt," but which is committed to removing slave labour from cocoa farms in West Africa and other regions, advocating equal and consistent fair pay. They distribute across the UK, Europe, and the US, and have a powerful community story where their primary goal is not financial success. As it says on the wrapper of their chocolate bars, their goal is "100% slave-free chocolate."

Oatly, a Sweden-based company valued at around $2 billion, is an up-and-coming oat milk brand that also has an environmentally sustainable story where their purpose is "to make it easy for people to turn what they eat and drink into personal moments of healthy joy, without recklessly taxing the planet's resources and processes." Oatly was founded in the 1990s and the company's patented enzyme technology copies nature's own process and turns oats into nutritional liquid food that is perfectly designed for humans. Investors have been flocking to the Oatly brand, including celebrities such as Oprah Winfrey, Natalie Portman, and the former Starbucks Chairman and CEO Howard Schultz.

So, it's clear that businesses are starting to wholeheartedly embrace community, social, and environmental value, which is being accepted with open arms by people around the world.

BUSINESS, FINANCIAL, AND DATA VALUE: It's vital to develop a strong business value proposition to derive value. With customers' rapidly changing needs, business products and services need to work with technology and data advancements so companies can keep doing what they're doing and ideally scale. Uber is a great example of a business that delivers a clear customer value proposition – getting people from A to B using your own car – and is scalable globally across a simple-to-use app.

The value of data in today's digital world cannot be underestimated. While there are varying views around data being valued on the balance sheet, the fact remains that data will be the fuel that drives businesses of the future.

In the World Bee Project example earlier in this chapter, the organisation partnered with a research university and Oracle, a platform business whose mission is to help people see data in new ways, discover insights, and unlock endless possibilities. Their network has the ability to scale, providing cloud-based solutions, machine learning, and cognitive AI capability that enable such a great initiative. As the data keeps flowing in, it provides more insights and potentially value as a result.

They created the world's first globally coordinated honeybee hive monitoring initiative, combining data from sensors and world-leading bee research with AI. None of this could have been possible five years ago. The cognitive automation, cloud capability, IoT, and ecosystem partnerships just simply didn't exist then. But a value-creation mindset and effectively leveraging new digital technology have led to a project that can have profound effects on the lives of people from all around the world.

BLUE-SKY THINKING AND CREATIVE PROBLEM SOLVING: Blue-sky thinking refers to thinking or brainstorming without limits – looking at a problem with fresh eyes. This kind of thinking is open to all creative ideas, regardless of immediate practical constraints. In the World Bee Project, by applying blue-sky thinking and creative problem solving, they were able to come up with a globally inspired project that's helping to better support some of the world's ecosystems.

As automation unshackles us, blue-sky thinking is an area that we can use to solve business challenges. Rather than just doing that project you've been wanting to implement for some time, you now have the opportunity to leapfrog into a different orbit and find really powerful, but perhaps non-traditional, solutions to your business needs. The development of the smartphone is a great example. In 2007, Steve Jobs, a founder of Apple, gave a keynote introducing the iPhone, a device that would change the way people around the world communicated. Aptly, Jobs began by saying, "Every once in a while, a revolutionary product comes along that changes everything."

Tesla is another great example of a business built from out-of-the-box thinking. Tesla was founded in 2003 by engineers. The main idea was to prove that electric cars could be as good as, if not better than, petrol and diesel car alternatives. When Elon Musk took over as a CEO, he started to roll out a competitive price strategy. Tesla's vision is to create the most compelling car company of the 21st century by driving the world's transition to electric vehicles. It is clear, compelling, inspirational and aligns to a social agenda of electric vehicles that ultimately will help undo the global negative impacts of fossil fuel emissions.

However, fear not: blue-sky thinking is not only for Steve Jobs and Elon Musk; any business can apply blue-sky thinking to disrupt a category, deliver a unique product or service, or rapidly grow market share.

Humans are generally really good at creative problem solving. It is what defines us and sets us apart from machines. Using the creative parts of our brains allows us to solve complex problems where a lateral solution may not be instantly obvious. Often, getting the right people together to workshop creative ideas is a great start. This combines many minds with different thinking styles to help work on a problem, allowing you to look at it from different angles.

Creative problem solving takes many forms. It could be reinventing a well-known service that has been around for centuries, like taxis, with an app-based business model like Uber. Or it could be taking a product like the motor car that has been around for a century and reinventing the engine to be more sustainable and eco-friendly without directly burning fossil fuels, like Tesla. Or it might simply be solving a revenue shortfall problem by implementing an RPA process in the fees and billing area to bring money in faster to reinvest on the short-term money market. Whatever the challenge, being open to thinking about problems creatively offers up endless possibilities.

By taking the robot out of the human, we can create space to explore opportunities that focus more on value-creation areas, helping to redirect human focus on things humans are best at, like creative problem solving, using empathy, connection, giving tactful advice, understanding, relationship building, blue-sky thinking, and so on. All of these go towards developing a value-creation mindset.

EXERCISE 5 – AMPLIFIED VALUE CREATION MINDSET SCORECARD

Developing long-term sustainable value that incorporates environmental, community and social value will be essential to thrive into the next decade. The exercise can be found at www.taketherobotoutofthehuman.com/exercises to help you identify where you're currently sitting and what areas you should focus on to amplify and further develop a value-creation mindset.

CASE STUDY – OCADO GROUP – MULTI BILLION DOLLAR UK TECH BUSINESS

Ocado Group is a publicly traded company that develops software, robotics, and automation systems for online retailers, with a net worth of over 21 billion dollars. Their purpose is to re-imagine shopping, by solving complex problems to provide sustainable solutions online. With state-of-the-art AI-fuelled robotic warehouse capability, they use their expertise and insight to enable partners to reduce their impact on the planet, whilst radically reducing the environmental impact of their own operations.

THE CHALLENGE: With over 7.6 trillion dollars globally as the potential market opportunity, Ocado Group's challenge was to drive significant increases in online penetration that shift behaviour away from visiting well established bricks-and-mortar grocery centres.

THE SOLUTION: With a clear amplified value-creation mindset, Ocado's focus extends to acting responsibly, resonating with social, communal, ethical and environmental considerations and current important global themes. Their group corporate responsibility strategy also aligns with several of the UN Sustainability Development Goals to save the planet and focuses on:

1. **Natural Resources,** where they use their expertise and insight to enable partners to reduce their impact on the planet. Their focus areas are:

   - Responding to the climate crisis and mapping their resource usage
   - Reducing the climate impact of their operations
   - Investing in new technologies and innovating for good

2. **Skills for the future,** where they share their skills and capabilities that will be needed tomorrow:

   - Enabling people to get on with their lives
   - Keeping communities and workplaces safe
   - Getting people online and helping build digital literacy

3. **Responsible sourcing,** where they put people first to create a positive impact across their ecosystem and supply chain:

   - Managing risk by mapping and assessing high-risk products and materials
   - Preventing modern slavery and tackling forced labour and human trafficking
   - A commitment to human rights within their supply chain

By executing the business strategy with an amplified value-creation mindset, they deliver long term value to shareholders across 4 pillars.

- **Society and community**: through technology, continually reducing environmental impacts, enabling market-leading food waste efficiency, near closed-loop recycling of plastic bags used in deliveries, and improved carbon efficiency – ultimately changing the way the world shops for good.
- **Partners**: offering flexible, scalable and efficient online grocery fulfilment, enabling them to grow, and investing in platforms, improvements and innovations to enhance a competitive advantage.
- **People**: making significant investments in recruiting and developing people who are passionate and of the highest quality.
- **Shareholders**: investing heavily to scale solutions to develop the platform and future value.

THE RESULTS:

Environment & Community: Ocado's Corporate Social Responsibility (CSR) / Environmental, Social, Governance (ESG) overall ranking is 52%, which is above the industry average. They have an ambition to be the UK's greenest, most innovative and best value grocery retailer.

- Closed-loop recycling: carrier bags from Ocado and other shops are recycled.
- Green van slots: customers can choose green van slots to minimise carbon impacts in delivery.
- Reducing food waste: food waste is sent to Biogen, who use waste to produce electricity and fertiliser. Food donations are also made to charity and staff discount shops.
- Peace One Day: a non-profit which is raising global awareness of Peace Day.
- Root Camp partnership: an organisation providing camping and cooking courses for teenagers.

- Waitrose Foundation & Prince's Charities Foundation: donations to help improve the lives of farm workers in South Africa, Ghana and Kenya and across 20 non-profit organisations.

Partners, Suppliers and Products: Ocado added 300 Technology colleagues in 2020, to meet the accelerated needs of partners whilst continuing to innovate on the capabilities of their platform. They opened Customer Fulfilment Centres (CFCs) in Paris and Toronto, and increased capacity in their UK CFCs, to enable Ocado Retail to serve as many customers as possible, with their facilities running at peak volumes through their warehouse in Erith. They materially increased partner volumes of in-store fulfilment through the platform, bringing operating levels to more than five times those seen at the beginning of 2020.

People: Ocado Group have a commitment to rewarding appropriately, engaging, listening to and developing employees. They offer share options to employees to own part of the business and a flexible modern work environment. They provide employees with the Mind Yourself mental health support programme with weekly check-in surveys, access to mental health champions, confidential networks for emotional support, and a global app to support well-being.

Financial: Ocado had a 1.7% share of UK grocery market in November 2020, up from 1.2% in November 2019, with UK take-home grocery sales up 11% over the same period. Revenue for the group in 2020 was up 32.7% to 2.3 billion pounds, and retail was up 35.3% to 2.1 billion pounds.

CHAPTER 6

PARTNERSHIPS AND ECOSYSTEMS

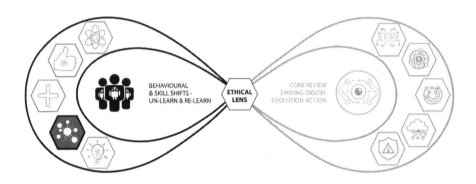

B uilding stronger partnerships across your organisation and more broadly across ecosystems can help enable businesses to be more effective in this new digital world. They expand a business's ability beyond its more traditional partner models and boundaries to better meet customer expectations, broaden innovation, and meet business goals through ecosystem partners.

But this requires a new way of thinking about partnerships. It means adapting your thinking to consider a broader, more connected way of partnering. In some respects, it may mean re-learning the fundamentals – considering things like integrated and centralised data across the organisation, taking a leadership role to partner across the business and integrate the vision and strategy, more widely exploring cross-industry partnerships, and building new organic business models to better meet the changing needs of your customers. By tapping into new technologies and different ways of thinking, and looking at non-traditional partnerships with businesses that in previous decades may even have been labelled competitors, businesses that are building effective ecosystem partnerships are well poised to thrive in the coming decades.

A simple example to demonstrate ecosystem partnerships in action is the set of partnerships involved in delivering the modern motor car. A few decades ago, cars didn't need wireless connectivity, sophisticated technology or computer chips, telecommunications connectivity, app integration, IoT, or cloud platform connections. There were a relatively small number of key partners needed to deliver a car, generally most within the motor industry and many located within the same country. However, today, the number of partners needed has grown due to advancing technology and increasing customer desires, where partnerships are often cross-industry and cross-country. The industries needed today include hardware and technology, IoT/cloud platforms, software and operating systems, WiFi-enabled telecommunications and connectivity, app platforms, connected insurance, and so on.

In this chapter, we'll explore partnerships and ecosystems, including some key dimensions that enable ecosystem partnerships, like:

- adopting design-disruptive thinking to introduce new thinking methodologies
- leveraging synaptic platforms to consider new partners across technology, cloud solutions, infrastructure partnerships, IoT APIs, and app collaborations
- cross-industry partnerships that you may not have previously considered
- blue-sky disrupters looking at out-of-the-box partnerships to disrupt and build scale

We'll then look at why this is important, and, finally, we'll explore how you can build this more robust partnership and ecosystem approach into your business.

WHAT ARE VALUABLE PARTNERSHIPS ACROSS YOUR BUSINESS AND BROADER ECOSYSTEMS?

Looking inside the business for a moment, as your business model starts to evolve from digitally naive to digitally mature, it shifts from siloed, rigid and robotic in processes and approach to more centralised, fluid and organic. As this evolution occurs, knowing how to build partnerships across the organisation will be important and requires a high degree of digitally savvy knowhow. Building these partnerships across the business requires that you have developed a high degree of Digital EQ so you can help lead your business, department, division or team to drive the right collaborations and solutions.

If your business is in the early phases of digital evolution – or at the starting on the track phase – you'll need to consider building partnerships across departmental siloes and try to unify and motivate teams with different agendas, ambitions, goals and possibly unlinked KPI's. This means working with the business owners and executive team to align outcomes and develop common integrated strategies. Where a lower degree of digital EQ exists, building trust in automation and different ways to deliver results will be important. If, however your business is more digitally mature, it's likely that you operate with cloud-based AI-fuelled platforms and a customer focus with centralised, integrated big data that drives business insights. So, working within this more agile business model means a different approach to developing nimble engagement, where teams are more digitally savvy with a greater appreciation for AI and a modern entrepreneurial spirit that embraces failure tolerance with an enhanced value-creation mindset. In each scenario, your partnership approach will need to be handled differently, based on the level of digital maturity and your levels of Digital EQ. Failing to develop successful partnerships across the business may negatively impact the outcomes your business has set in this new digital age. However, with careful assessment, empathy, and building your Digital EQ, you can forge strong partnerships across the business to drive the results you desire.

Looking outside the business to building broader ecosystem partnerships means exploring partnerships in a different way. Simply put, a business ecosystem is a network of cross-industry businesses who work together to deliver customer solutions. As customer solutions more and more require greater digital capability, the ecosystems become broader and deeper and are now technology platform-based. Partner ecosystems a decade ago were a vastly different landscape to partner ecosystems today, where each partner can now deliver a piece of the consumer solution or contribute a necessary capability and the value the ecosystem generates is larger than the combined value each business could contribute individually. In some respects, ecosystem partnerships today may be non-traditional, unexpected, internationally based, or may even expand across different business sectors to better complement your business.

We've touched on why it's really important to have a human (customer) approach to building your business in previous chapters; however, driving customer value is absolutely vital and you need to keep it sitting at the very centre of your ecosystem partnership strategy. Knowing what your customer wants and needs, how they want to receive your product or service, and what makes a highly valued customer journey will help shape your ecosystem partnership selection. If you build it right, customer satisfaction should translate back into business value and growth.

For example, Amazon was looking to improve the way small businesses sell on their platform, so they partnered with American Express on a co-branded credit card. This card helps users buy goods, but also provides enhanced data insights on their purchasing activity. This partnership highlights the need to understand your customer, their needs, and what drives their satisfaction, thereby ensuring you have the optimal experience in place to grow your business. These insights are what inform the framework for your partner ecosystem strategy, as well as ensuring it thrives.

I recently met with the CEOs from two prominent global professional accounting bodies, CA ANZ and ACCA, who recently formed a ground-breaking strategic alliance for their industry. Together, these two organisations pooled their thought leadership resources, respective market share strengths, global office infrastructure, and continued lifelong learning professional development (CPD) programmes. This enhanced the professional experience and knowledge pool of their combined 870,000 members, as well as future professional accounts, in over 180 countries around the world.

Rick Ellis, CA ANZ's former Chief Executive, said that he had seen significant progress as a result of the alliance.

> *Aligning of the ACCA and CA ANZ brands is having a positive impact on the standing of the profession, particularly in Asia, and this is consistent with our government's focus on strengthening trade and ties in this region.*
>
> —Rick Ellis, former CEO, CA ANZ

ACCA's Chief Executive, Helen Brand, agreed, highlighting that the two bodies' pooled resources resulted in joint reports such as the 'G20 public trust in tax' responsibilities for financial reporting: what you need to know." She also went on to say that together, their voice and influence is stronger.

> *The alliance represents the voice of 870,000 members and future professional accountants around the world, who share the commitment to uphold the highest ethical, professional, and technical standards. Sharing our expertise and combining our resources allows us to strengthen our reach and relevance. It also enables us to provide better support and resources to members and other stakeholders.*
>
> —Helen Brand, Chief Executive, ACCA

What's interesting about these two organisations is that, prior to this alliance, they were effectively global competitors. However, each respective CEO had the foresight to recognise the benefits of looking outside their normal sphere of partnerships. By thinking outside the box, they formed an alliance that enabled them to do more together than apart, delivering more value to their members by extension. Their combined voice on the world stage was amplified and enhanced their ability to influence on core policy issues impacting the accounting profession. Together they also formed numerous other unique, dynamic partnerships, such as one with KPMG on relevant thought leadership around Robotics Process

Automation in Finance. The alliance had challenged old-style concepts about professional accountancy bodies working together, giving the combined voices of the two organisations much greater combined weight.

Another example of broader ecosystem partnership is the one between Walt Disney World Resorts and Hitachi Vantara, who have recently brought together Disney's entertainment experience and Hitachi Vantara's intelligent, data-driven solutions to increase the attractions' operational efficiency and appeal to customers.

As we can see, ecosystem partnerships can take many shapes. They can exist as alliances between seemingly competitive businesses – technology businesses partnering with entertainment businesses and online ordering businesses with financial institutions.

WHY DEVELOP PARTNERSHIPS ACROSS YOUR BUSINESS AND BROADER ECOSYSTEMS?

Why should you care about any of this? Won't the Executive Directors or Department Heads take care of integrating the strategy and driving the business forward through your business digital evolution? In relation to building the right ecosystem partnerships, won't the contracts department, procurement teams, legal teams, marketing, logistics, or sales departments take care of this? The digital tide is moving so fast that if you don't take a leadership stance and develop an understanding and a different approach to building partnerships in this new digital age, you run the risk of delivering a less than optimal service or product in the eyes of your customers. With the role of professional accountants, business and finance leaders shifting towards driving strategy and enhanced value creation, it is essential to help lead this and ensure that the public and business interest is served.

Today, the heightened customer expectations to get an intuitive experience, timely service, and near-instant fulfilment, coupled with the rapidly evolving technology platforms, are fuelling the need for continuous and ongoing digital transformations across businesses. As processes, products, and services evolve, enterprises are looking beyond the business-as-usual (BAU) norms that worked well in past decades and are now casting their gaze to broader, more dynamic partnerships, alliances, and collaborations that harness different business models, utilise disruptive design thinking, provide a big data customer-centric focus, broaden new markets and platforms, and ideally gain a more sustainable competitive edge to stay relevant.

Many companies across the world are also eagerly exploring partnerships beyond conventional boundaries to find scale, connectivity, or greater competitive advantage, or simply due to the need to reinvent and stay relevant in rapidly shifting times.

The use of new technology and dynamic ecosystems are self-evident in the new car manufacturing process. For example, since 2018, the BMW Group has been using AI applications in car production, relieving staff of repetitive inspection tasks. Take, for example, automated image recognition. In these processes, BMW uses cameras to take pictures of the car components, revealing potential micro-cracks. The AI compares them in milliseconds to hundreds of other images of the same sequence. This way, the AI application can identify deviations in real time and checks whether all parts have been mounted in the right place.

In the health sector, ecosystem partnerships are being used more and more. AI uses are increasing in areas such as improving radiology diagnoses, making MedTech devices smart, and identifying new infection patterns. All of these results are only possible with the use of broader ecosystem partnerships.

In 2019, UPS began conducting a trial programme called Flight Forward, using autonomous drone deliveries of critical medical samples, including blood or tissue. The FAA granted the company approval to expand to hospitals around the US over the coming years. So, by using their traditional delivery service model, now leveraging a new ecosystem partner to power autonomous drone delivery, they took their business to another level.

There are countless other examples, such as TeiaCare, a healthtech startup that's developed a digital monitoring technology, and Ancelia, which uses artificial intelligence and intelligent video analytics to assist nurses in the care of elderly patients. Founded in 2018, TeiaCare uses an optical sensor, positioned on the ceiling above the bed, to monitor specific movements and resting positions, detecting changes and deteriorations where it sends alerts directly to carers. Without the help of ecosystem partnerships, this type of medical breakthrough and customer solutions would not be possible.

Paris-based Dreem call themselves "sleep pioneers". They've developed wearable headsets that gather data on how you sleep (brain waves, heart rate, respiratory rate, etc.) and recommend how you can sleep better. Each morning, users can see a review of their night's sleep via the app, including things like what position they slept in. Combining science, technology, and design, Dreem has had support from investors and gained government grants to help people solve sleep disorders – a growing health and societal problem today. Again, these breakthroughs would not be possible without ecosystem partners that span science, technology, and design.

In the finance sector, ecosystem partnerships are taking finance to the next level. Walmart partnered with Silicon Valley-based financial technology startups Even and PayActiv to launch a tool for personal money management, financial planning, and on-demand access to earned wages. Walmart developed a suite of financial wellness services for more than 1.4 million associates nationwide. Associates access the tools through the Even app, available on iOS and Android devices. "Every American worker faces unexpected and stressful between-paychecks expenses," said Safwan Shah, founder and CEO of PayActiv. "With on-demand access to earned wages, Walmart associates will be able to save more, avoid the financial traps that reduce their take-home pay, and get a level of stability that few service sector employers provide."

Global accounting and consultancy network BDO reported double-digit growth over twelve months, recording figures of $9.6 billion for its 2019 financial year. With some twenty purchases made, BDO has been strategically pursuing an inorganic strategy to augment its capabilities in areas such as cybersecurity and digital solutions. Rather than partnerships, they've opted to broaden business capability through acquisitions, including boutique Australian cloud accounting and business advisory Consolid8, and consultancies Lootok and Global Trade Strategies (GTS) in the US. By acquiring businesses with sought-after digital capability, they have been able to broaden and improve their client solutions.

Ecosystem partnerships are a vital part of building and developing sustainable, digitally transformed businesses. The good news is that the more effective your partnerships are, the more effective your business will become. But it can sometimes be a little confusing where to start and how to go about developing these.

HOW CAN I DEVELOP PARTNERSHIPS ACROSS BROADER ECOSYSTEMS?

To help frame up effective ecosystem partnerships, the asset below shows the key areas to focus on to help your business grow and thrive.

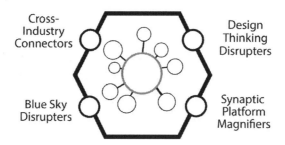

Often, it's good to start by looking more closely at your existing partnerships, where you may find they have other capabilities, connections, and services that you were not aware of and could mutually benefit from exploring further. Doing an audit of existing partnerships across your business is a good way to unearth this. Sometimes you may find there are duplications and inefficiencies when you look across the business. The benefit, however, of working with existing partners with new untapped partnership potential is that is you may already have a good working relationship and a strong cultural fit, giving you an immediate advantage to build on the relationship further. If this is not the case, then a new partnership may be worth exploring. Finding partners who complement and align to your business is key, so it's important to make sure you have a clear selection, performance, and service-level framework that supports your business objectives, culture, and brand. The importance of working with partners that share similar cultural, attitudinal, and business rhythms cannot be underestimated, so having this in your selection criteria is worth considering beyond typical business and service metrics.

CROSS-INDUSTRY CONNECTORS: Identifying the gaps between your business strategy, customer satisfaction, and value proposition should start to shed some light on what type of ecosystem partnerships will add value. When you look at the products or experiences your customers expect today, and map this against your current customer journey, you're likely to see gaps that can be improved upon (unless you already deliver exceptional customer service like Apple or Netflix). As a result, you may need to look more broadly at suppliers and distributors from different market sectors, even competitors, if there are complementary benefits or collaborations with businesses in other markets. Cross-industry connectors include delivery, service, content, and solution partners.

I recall working with the Sydney Olympic Games Organising Committee to deliver the Sydney Olympic Games, where almost all of the partner programmes were across industry sectors. These included facilities, airlines, media, banking, and medical, to help fund and deliver the Olympic Games. This cross-industry partner ecosystem helped to deliver a better overall customer experience. IBM was the technology partner providing the web capability and systems that delivered fast and accurate results from each event. Swatch were the timekeepers, Panasonic supplied screens, BHP provided steel construction materials, infrastructure, and engineering services, Energy Australia provided power, and so on. All of these were required to deliver the Olympic Games and enable a great customer experience.

DESIGN THINKING DISRUPTERS: In business today, companies need to look beyond the traditional partner or supplier pool. There have been big gains in the use of such partnerships as corporate venture capital, incubators, and accelerators to meet growing customer needs. A recent Boston

Consulting Group report on innovative companies found that companies were working more with incubator hubs to improve their businesses. The use of incubators rose from 59% in 2015 to 75% in 2018. Further, companies were developing academic relationships much faster, which jumped from 60% to 81% during the same period. Finally, the report showed that the over-all formation of partnerships was on the rise from 65% to 83%, to support the growing customer and business needs.

The Optus Macquarie University Cyber Security Hub is a great example of uni-versities and corporate working together. Optus, the wholly owned subsidiary of Singtel, made a commitment to train up thousands of its employees to be more cybersecurity savvy. They formed a joint partnership with Macquarie University to develop the Cyber Security Hub, with an aim to train the next generation of cybersecurity specialists. The Hub endeavours to raise awareness among business leaders and develop the skills of businesses today through tackling real-world challenges in cybersecurity. The Hub offers a platform for exchange between academics and practitioners from business and government, along with conducting research across multiple disciplines, such as computing, engineering, business, criminology, law, and psychology.

Many other universities, including Oxford University, have a startup incubator to support entrepreneurs. The Oxford University startup incubator is aimed at en-trepreneur-driven ventures that are not university spinouts. With backing from MBA alumnus Bryan Morton, entrepreneur and CEO of Oxford Therapeutics, the Centre for Entrepreneurship at the University of Durham champions the StartGrid Accelerator programme, which is another great incubator initiative.

If you Google "business incubators for startups and entrepreneurs," at least 150 results pop up that are UK-based alone, and the number is growing. This only further demonstrates that new businesses with new ways of thinking, new tech, and new business models that can potentially disrupt well-established businesses are on the rise. Looking to partner with startups, accelerators, or universities can bring fresh business approaches to the table from a lean, agile, and frugal innovation perspective. Partnerships and collaborations with startups can also broaden your brand image for not only customers, but the people that work with you. This will, in turn, open up new ways to build and develop customer data.

When you attempt to solve problems with the same methodology that you have always used, you will almost always end up with the same results. In our Global Head of Funds Management example in Chapter 2, they trialled university students in their process re-design phase for an RPA project to bring a fresh perspective and different way of thinking about problems and solutions in an automated world. As digital natives and design thinkers, they provided a fresh pair of eyes for the business teams to help them develop more sustainable processes and solutions for automation. When I recently spoke to the Global Head of Funds Management about the project, he went on to say that "it really helped the business teams to think differently about what the processes would be in an automated world." He took it a step further and ensured that he put the engineers, IT teams, and accountants together to collaborate and work together to find useful solutions. He finished by saying, "You can't just replicate a process for automation. You need to disrupt the norm and apply design thinking to refine how the automation process will work best in the future." This example conveys that, often, disrupting the way that we normally do things can yield some tremendous results, whether by using a shadow board to get a fresh perspective on a set of challenges, or by bringing in university students to transform business processes.

A recent 2019 Harvard Business Review article titled "Why You Should Create a Shadow Board Including Younger Employees" outlined the exponential value that can be derived from using a shadow board. A shadow board often consists of a group of digital-savvy Gen Y or Zs that can provide a fresh perspective to traditional problems. It further conveyed how companies like Prada and Gucci have utilised shadow boards of groups of non-executive employees that work with senior executives on strategic initiatives to leverage the younger group's insights and help broaden and diversify perspectives. The outcomes of such initiatives have been overwhelmingly positive, where, for example, Gucci's revenue and market growth was attributed to their internet and digital strategies.

When I spoke with the Dean of Business at Durham University, she was very supportive and encouraging of the shadow board approach, stating:

> *Creating shadow boards, where students come with a different way of looking at problems, could really add value to help positively disrupt legacy business challenges. We have loads of bright young people, who are curious and look at new ways of doing things. They come to study what they love and look at things through a different lens to that of older generations.*
>
> —Susan Hart, Executive Dean of Business,
> Durham University

SYNAPTIC PLATFORM MAGNIFIERS: These are platforms that help businesses develop deeper digital solutions to meet growing customer needs. As we move towards a big-data, connected world, it will be important to ensure that partners, platforms, and projects have big-data, connected, and scalable capability. A good example of this is the World Bee Project, who used big-data, IoT, data analytics, and the cloud to find solutions to the alarming drop in bee population globally. One of their partners was Oracle, who were able to leverage their diverse and in-depth ecosystem. By combining data from sensors in the Global Hive Network and world-leading bee research with AI, they can generate and access new insights that can help inform and implement global actions to improve pollinator habitats, create more sustainable ecosystems, and improve food security, nutrition, and livelihoods.

With the rising expectations of customers that are now only satisfied through digital big-data solutions, having sound, synaptic partners will be essential. The platform capabilities that are available today are staggering and they will only become more powerful and interconnected. Factoring them into your ecosystem partner framework will be pivotal as your business grows.

BLUE SKY DISRUPTERS: A disruption by definition can be defined as a disturbance, which interrupts an event, activity, process, or market. Regardless of whether your brand is established or new, with the unprecedented amount of promotional noise in the world today from millions of brands across every category, partnering with businesses that help you create a category disruption is a way to get your brand or business to get noticed and stay relevant.

In a recent survey of over 1200 business leaders from diverse industries around the world, it was found that 60% of executives were of the view that building ecosystems will disrupt their industry.

> *60% of executives said building ecosystems would disrupt their industry, where nearly half have already built, or are currently building, ecosystems to respond to disruption.*

A category disrupter can be any business or brand in any category that, when combined with your business, delivers exponential value to your customers. Finding a category disrupter ecosystem partnership often requires out-of-the-box or blue-sky thinking, but, if you can identify one, will provide a material point of difference, as well as a valuable, competitive edge. For example, a recent Adidas partnership with rapper Kanye West in 2019 saw Adidas' net income climb 19.5% to $1.9 billion.

Another example of a category disrupter is the LEGO and Emmet.ai partnership. As a result of the latter, you can now use AI to turn photos on your phone into virtual LEGO, subsequently creating a parts list as well as building instructions so that you can build Master Builder quality LEGO models, rewarding your physical LEGO play with digital LEGO experiences. This new initiative further enables users to transform themselves into customisable LEGO mini figures. LEGO's partnership with Emmet.ai is a game changer in their category.

However, developing the right partnerships and knowing where to start can often be a little daunting. So how do you go about doing this?

EXERCISE 6 – PARTNERSHIPS & ECOSYSTEMS – SCORE CARD

A good ecosystem partnership strategy today could be the difference between a hugely successful business and one that disappears, so it's vital to start thinking about this in relation to your specific business and market category from the customers' viewpoint and in a non-traditional way. Download this exercise at www.taketherobotoutofthehuman.com/exercises to help frame your thinking around finding the right ecosystem partnerships, looking at your existing relationships and/or new ones.

CHAPTER 7

ENTREPRENEURIAL (MODERN) SPIRIT

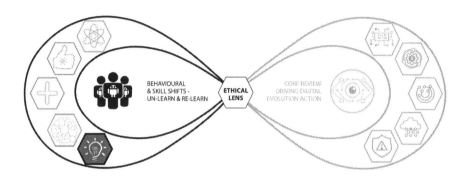

T o thrive and get ahead of the curve in this new, big data-centric world, it's essential to develop a modern entrepreneurial spirit. In a recent conversation, a past President of IFAC and a major bank transformation leader referred to her well-established bank as a "202-year-old startup." Even though you don't readily associate a 202-year-old bank with a startup, this was clearly the way they have reinvented their approach – to adopt an entrepreneurial spirit.

> *Some startups are ahead of their time. Others don't have enough controls. Some grow too big, too quickly and don't have sufficient processes or controls in place, of which you need a combination. To be more effective, we need to communicate with our teams and bring people on the journey. Develop trust and have an entrepreneurial spirit.*
>
> —Rachel Grimes, Past President of IFAC

Many universities around the world have developed entrepreneurial programmes for the business leaders of tomorrow, capitalising on and nurturing the natural curiosity of Generations Y and Z. Oxford University has the Oxford Centre for Innovation and numerous entrepreneurial programmes. Cambridge has developed a Master of Studies in Entrepreneurship focusing on developing impactful entrepreneurs. Durham University's business school has an entire faculty focused on entrepreneurship, incorporating incubator hubs in their programme of learning, where science and technology are knitting into their programmes with a strong focus on business startups. In the words of the Dean of Business:

> *It's vital to have an entrepreneurial spirit. This allows our students, the business leaders of tomorrow, to be more flexible, build on their curiosity, and more able to deal with ongoing and continuous change.*

> —Susan Hart, Executive Dean of Business Durham University

Right now, businesses are trying to make sense of how new AI-fuelled technology, big data cloud-based analytics, cybersecurity, and vast-reaching new ecosystems can be leveraged to stay relevant in the eyes of their customers and stakeholders. One of the challenges that many businesses face in staying relevant is the need to evolve from older business models, older technology, and older mindsets that matched these practices. This means embracing a different way of operating, thinking, and behaving to be more relevant in a digital age, which can be quite a daunting task.

The good news is that building a modern entrepreneurial spirit does not mean throwing caution to the wind, being reckless, or taking excessive risks. It means applying modern entrepreneurial traits to better navigate the rapid shifts, twists, and turns that are coming thick and fast at businesses and individuals today. In this chapter, we'll look at core principles that will help you build a stronger modern entrepreneurial spirit by taking an experimental approach to testing, re-testing, and reviewing, as well as adopting a healthy failure tolerance; by leading with courage and being a real force for galvanising business teams and projects; and by being adaptable and applying dynamic risk-using data to drive insights to enable a more informed position. We'll then look at why this is important, and finally, we'll explore how you can build an entrepreneurial spirit.

A QUICK TRIP DOWN MEMORY LANE

Despite technology's rapid vault forwards, sometimes it's good to pause and take stock by looking backwards at the fundamentals. At the turn of the last century, Henry Ford, founder of the Ford Motor Company, was considered to be one of the greatest entrepreneurs of his time. He was at the cutting edge of industry by mass-producing automobiles to make affordable cars more accessible to more people. His dream was to create an automobile that everyone could afford. The Model T made this dream a reality. By bringing this vision to life, he set in motion the demise of the horse, cart, and buggy and helped set the stage for robotic automation a century later. Ford also became extremely wealthy, reaching a billion-dollar business by 1925. As such, his traits and behaviours have been noted as those of the classic entrepreneur – persistent, visionary, adaptable, determined, experimental, and a risk taker.

Joseph Schumpeter, a well-known economist of the first half of the twentieth century, developed an entrepreneurial definition which certainly fits entrepreneurs like Henry Ford.

> *The function of entrepreneurs is to reform or revolutionise the pattern of production by exploiting an invention or, more generally, an untried technological possibility for producing a new commodity or producing an old one in a new way, by opening up a new source of supply of materials or a new outlet for products, by reorganising an industry and so on. The entrepreneur is a pioneer who is able to act with confidence beyond the range of familiar beacons. His characteristic task, theoretically as well as historically, consists precisely in breaking up old, and creating new, tradition.*
>
> —Joseph Schumpeter

Henry Ford emulated this definition and was quoted at the turn of the century.

> *Be ready to revise any system, scrap any method, abandon any theory, if the success of the job requires it.*
>
> —Henry Ford

Ford's quote is as true today as it was a century ago, despite the fact that the technology landscape is radically different. You've only got to search some of the more prominent startup hubs to see these new forms of digital cognitive businesses are springing up in every industry. For example, businesses like Stitch Fix deliver styling services and clothing direct to women based on both their preferences and through analysing choices made by other customers. Coupa enables companies to optimise their purchasing processes, subsequently saving cost and improving quality. Rubicon Global created a virtual, national waste-hauling and recycling network for businesses. Iora Health has a different model for primary care that improves health outcomes at lower costs – and the list goes on.

Today's workforce is already made up of bots and humans working side by side, drones distributing medical supplies to hard-to-reach areas, autonomous cars and machine-driven manufacturing, the birth of the metaverse and cognitive systems analysing trillions of data points to improve heightened customer experiences on the road to true AI; it's a very different world to the one Henry Ford lived in. So, what then makes up the modern entrepreneurial traits or spirit that is needed to navigate all this?

WHAT IS A MODERN ENTREPRENEURIAL SPIRIT?

While some people still associate entrepreneurship with startups, risk takers, and visionaries who disrupt traditional business models, the truth is you don't need to lead a multibillion-dollar business to embody a modern entrepreneurial spirit. Many people I've spoken with described "entrepreneurial" using words like **visionary, innovative, passionate, risk taker**, and **creative**. I can certainly think of many well-known entrepreneurs who fit this profile, such as Richard Branson, founder of the Virgin Group; Jeff Bezos, founder of Amazon; Sergey

Brin and Larry Page, co-founders of Google; Susan Wojcicki, CEO of YouTube; Sarah Blakely, founder of Spanx; Elon Musk, founder of SpaceX and CEO of Tesla; Walt Disney, co-founder of the Walt Disney company; Steve Jobs, co-founder of Apple; Henry Ford, founder of Ford Motors; Debbie Fields, founder of Mrs Fields Bakeries; Cher Wang, co-founder of HTC; Denise Coates, founder of Bet365; and the list goes on.

This traditional entrepreneurial view is evolving as new technology fuels the new era, where adapting to rapid change is becoming business as usual. In a recent study of over 2000 millennials, almost 60% classified themselves as entrepreneurs and 90% of professionals surveyed indicated that being an entrepreneur today means having a certain mindset. This study suggested that we should replace the typical definition of an entrepreneur, as someone who starts a company, with a newer definition – one based on the *mindset* of a person who sees opportunities and persistently pursues them.

The definition I prefer for a modern entrepreneurial spirit is galvanising success through solving problems that balance dynamic risk with reward; able to adapt, improvise, and overcome new challenges with a courageous, ethical, and confident manner through a curious, open-minded, and experimental approach.

I've spoken with many successful business leaders and pioneers who demonstrate a modern entrepreneurial spirit. Many don't consider themselves as overly creative. Many don't see themselves as visionaries or innovative. This, of course, is encouraging, given that most of us are not necessarily intrinsically innovative, visionaries, creative, or naturally comfortable taking huge risks. Instead, they consider themselves ordinary people who are committed to doing things well that matter to them. They are people who demonstrate courage and standing up for their vision and beliefs even if it's not the easy path, being adaptable in rapidly changing times, able to adapt, improvise, and overcome obstacles, having an experimental approach to testing and re-testing hypotheses with a healthy failure tolerance needed to support change, and, finally, having a dynamic risk approach that is supported by data insights to help make more informed decisions. Some may not have even used the term entrepreneur, but many demonstrate modern-day entrepreneurial traits, behaviours, and spirit. So, the question is, then, how can you further develop a modern entrepreneurial spirit?

HOW CAN YOU DEVELOP A MODERN ENTREPRENEURIAL SPIRIT?

A good starting point is not to be phased by the more typical perception of "entrepreneurial" and accept that the modern entrepreneurial behaviours are things that people are doing every day. It's just about flexing and building those muscles that help you become more adaptive and effective to the new, more digitally orientated ways of working.

Salesforce, a cloud-based software company headquartered in the US and generating over $17 billion in revenue, is a global business that provides customer relationship management service and a complementary suite of enterprise applications focused on customer service, marketing automation, analytics, and application development. Salesforce finds individuals with an entrepreneurial spirit by using a test at interview stage, giving them a project to showcase a product launch to demonstrate creativity, innovation, and entrepreneurial thinking. As entrepreneurship and creative leadership are a large part of Salesforce's work culture, this exercise helps business leaders to determine if new hires possess that entrepreneurial drive and the teamwork skills to work well with others.

The key to embodying a modern entrepreneurial spirit is gradually building stronger entrepreneurial muscles. It's no different from going to the gym or going for a run, walk, cycle, or swim to get fit. You need to work out what you want to achieve, what your goals are and what obstacles you need to overcome. Then, work out how you're going to get fit and build a plan that fits your lifestyle to do this. This usually means shifting from your usual, less active routine to a new and more demanding regime. You will then need to monitor your progress along the way and make adjustments as needed to stay on track. Building entrepreneurial behaviour is no different; you need to identify where you are now and build a plan to shift gears to where you want to be.

Adopting a modern entrepreneurial spirit doesn't mean throwing caution to the wind or suddenly taking on huge, uncharacteristic risks. It's about adopting the essence of an entrepreneur and those behaviours that work best in a more fluid, digital world and fit your own personal style. One award-winning CFO-turned-CEO I met with has a very clear view of what the modern entrepreneurial spirit looks like.

> *In today's rapidly changing world, you really need an agile entrepreneurial approach to business and a more commercially developed lens around risk in particular. I've found you need a trial-and-error mindset where you're willing to experiment with new things and not be afraid to fail. It takes courage to do this, but, with AI on our doorsteps, we need to take the leap.*
>
> —Paula Kensington, CEO PK Advisory

The CEO of another global accounting organisation shared a similar view.

> *The firms that are doing the best are the ones exhibiting an entrepreneurial spirit.*
>
> —Steve Heathcote, CEO, PrimeGlobal

Another Executive Director of a global professional accounting body defined entrepreneurial spirit as:

> *Identifying the opportunity, seizing that opportunity, identifying what your customers want and acting nimbly to deliver. It's about capturing the essence of entrepreneurial and applying it.*
>
> —Maggie McGhee, Executive Director, ACCA Global

After speaking with many business and finance leaders and digital pioneers, common behaviours and principles emerged. The asset below outlines these six key principles and behaviours that, when used in combination, help you build a modern entrepreneurial spirit.

ASSET 7.1: ENTREPRENEURIAL (MODERN) SPIRIT – DIMENSIONS

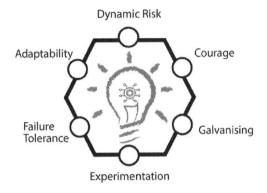

DYNAMIC RISK: One term that seems consistently associated with entrepreneurship is risk. However, everyone defines and confronts risk differently, with most seeking reward and trying to minimise or manage risk. The relationship between risk and reward is generally that without risk, there is no return, and without return, you shouldn't take on the risk. This doesn't mean jumping blindly into action. Instead, it's the opposite. Those with a developed entrepreneurial spirit make calculated moves while understanding that success is not always guaranteed. Successful risk management implies the ability to work autonomously and decisively, within higher degrees of ambiguity as new technologies flood into the market. Dynamic risk management involves balancing uncertainty surrounding risk versus reward, as well as having a risk tolerance that is tempered against a fluid, agile business dynamic. By ensuring that you have the right foundations, including the right people, you can capitalise on market opportunities. In a digital world, you must develop a good eye for pattern recognition to help recognise and better predict future marketplace trends.

SHIFT FROM RISK-AVERSE TO DYNAMIC RISK MANAGEMENT: The key is to shift from a more risk-averse, inflexible way of operating into a more dynamic one that grows as the business digitally transforms. This involves minimising risk by establishing more certainty around metrics through richer data by looking not just at the numbers, but also at the people, data, technology, ecosystem partnership opportunities, and market viability. Furthermore, understanding new technologies and methodologies like RPA, centralised base data lakes, cybersecurity solutions and platforms, as well as the impacts of these systems on your business, will give you a top line gauge and insights on areas you can work on.

COURAGE: One of my personal favourite entrepreneurs, in the more classic sense, was Walt Disney – a man who changed the animation industry with a unique perspective and a magical disposition. He was once quoted saying:

> *Courage is the main quality of leadership, in my opinion, no matter where it is exercised. Usually it implies some risk, especially in new undertakings.*
>
> —Walt Disney

Having the courage and certainty to stand firm and back your ideas, plans, and projects will be vital in this era of business disruption. As we move into uncharted waters, having a clear vision and certainty that your approach is sound is the first step, but having courage and conviction in your execution will be the key to bringing your teams, executives, and boards along the journey.

Persistence also goes hand in hand with courage. At Airbnb, the founders initially struggled to get traction. Eventually, the team joined a well-respected venture acceleration programme and figured out how to attract committed customers, which enabled them to attract capital, and helped create one of the most successful entrepreneurial ventures in history. In another example of persistence, Scott Cook founded Intuit in 1983 to sell personal financial management software called Quicken. Fast forward to 2020, and Intuit is a publicly traded company with over 7,000 employees and a market capitalisation of $79.4 billion. The company is best known for QuickBooks, a business accounting software service, and TurboTax, which helps consumers, small businesses, and tax professionals navigate the complex global tax system. Intuit struggled in the early days to find product market fit. However, with persistence, unwavering courage, and holding to their vision, they were successful.

SHIFT TO BECOMING MORE COURAGEOUS: In our case study in Chapter 2, the Global Head of Funds Management was running a team of professional accountants to oversee the financial fees and billing processes. While the processes at that time were manual and repetitive, they were working fine. His executive team initially asked the question, "Why change things if there is a risk of potential negative impacts on customers by developing an RPA project, when the current system is delivering?" By demonstrating courage, he was able to build the foundation of trust.

> *You must take the first step, which requires courage. It does take a leap of faith for other people to trust you and give you the opportunity to make this change. It came with some challenges. From a people point of view, some thought they were going to lose their jobs. From a management point of view, they said that I already have ten people looking after a very important area. So why change?*
>
> —Ali Mehfooz, Global Head of Funds Management, AMP Capital

He was convinced that the RPA project was the right approach. He knew the benefits through a robust business case and proof of concept and by exercising courage and conviction, he was able to convince all concerned. So, it's important to develop a certainty and conviction in your vision. Back yourself and have a clearly defined strategy and a belief in what you're doing to build and maintain trust.

GALVANISING: Modern entrepreneurs need to lead and inspire teams to work better together. It's about lighting the spark and bringing people to work together effectively, to galvanise collaboration and create a strong, unified culture. Galvanisers can take many forms. When people are genuinely passionate about the problems, they are energised by a challenge and that energy is contagious. Or some people may be good at communicating with others and have well-developed emotional intelligence. They know how to reach people, subsequently helping them to work effectively with other departments that speak an entirely different business language, or where humans now need to work with bots, both assisted and autonomously. They break down the siloes and help teams work together, despite the structure, by inspiring and motivating people to do the best they can. This can be as simple as capturing their trust or respect, or igniting their imagination through a clear vision to be part of something bigger than themselves. They help boards and leaders adopt a unified digital transformation strategy. They are good collaborators and digitally empathetic, leading change and helping to bridge the generational gaps between the older generations (Gen X and Baby Boomers) and the newer generations (Gen Y, Z, and Alpha). Capitalising on the invaluable experience from the older generations and the new ways of digital thinking by new generations is paramount. The modern entrepreneur galvanises and helps to bring all the elements together, building curiosity and inspiring contagious momentum within people by extension.

GALVANISING TEAMS: Enabling your teams to work better together, particularly if your structure is siloed, helps to build trust and galvanise a culture of collaboration. I interviewed a senior transformation leader at one of the major Australian banks with revenues of over $20 billion and a well-defined customer-centric digital transformation strategy. They were able to reduce operating costs by simplifying processes through digital technologies, creating more seamless digital experiences for customers in tandem. Her view on how to galvanise a team through an RPA implementation was:

> When we implemented the RPA project, rather than redundancy it was about redirection of people. As people move through this process, they realise the capacity they have to improve themselves, to see what's in it for them. So, having a robot free up that time gives them back those hours. To build trust, I told the CFO to say that no one will lose their job because of this. There was not a lot of belief, but in two years of running the programme, no one has lost their job. What's happened is people are saying now, 'my life has never been better.'
>
> —Rachel Grimes, Past President of IFAC

EXPERIMENTATION: In this new digital era, it's vital to think more like a scientist – to experiment to see what delivers the best outcome; to be agile and data-centric, and anticipate pivots both planned and unplanned; to have the approach where you test, re-test, and use proof of concepts to develop ideas rapidly to keep improving. Learning all the time from feedback, which is now much more available through new digital platforms and big data, facilitates this agility. Leaders today must be nimble and expect failure more readily as part of the process, rather than seeing it as something to be avoided and discouraged. Move away from doing things the way you always have because they worked in the past; seek instead the best customer experience or most sustainable business process you can build. As the convergence of factors that we read about in Chapter 1 continues to drive business model change, it's important that we evolve and adapt as well. Although some of us may not be used to the new pace, an experimental approach will drive better results.

GET EXPERIMENTAL: In considering agile competitors without cumbersome legacy systems, the promise of big data and customer centricity, more agile business models, and a more organic organisational structure, having an experimental approach will be a necessity. Testing and re-testing, using proof-of-concept prototypes, and conducting continuous research to improve experiences will be the new BAU. Accepting failure as part of the process rather than rejecting failure will be the new norm. Applying agile, SCRUM methodologies with newly found big data that is analysed by cognitive bots to verify how the customer experience can be improved will also become BAU. Many digitally geared retail organisations and mature digital businesses like Netflix are already doing this well; however, if you're just starting or on your way on the digital transformation curve, there is loads of room for smart experimentation in your business. In our major Australian bank example, the transformation leader found that as her team started to get more comfortable with the RPA platforms and develop more trust, she was able to encourage the teams to come up with new ways of improving processes and experiences themselves. As the teams became more curious, they began to experiment themselves as a result.

FAILURE TOLERANCE: In a world where people typically strive for success and shy from failure, we need to think differently and embrace failure as a powerful and necessary learning tool.

> *Failure is simply the opportunity to begin again, this time more intelligently.*
>
> —Henry Ford

The secret to finding opportunity is to be curious and willing to run experiments, with a high likelihood that things won't always work, at least in the beginning. You must be accepting of failure, because in a digital world where businesses will be fuelled by big data, nimble testing and re-testing will be the norm. Accordingly, Thomas Edison, the inventor of the light bulb, has often been quoted as having said, "I haven't failed, I've just found ten thousand ways that won't work."

By seeing failure as a way to inform and improve, Thomas Edison and his team trialled thousands of light bulbs and filaments until they found the right combination. By accepting failure as a way of learning and improving, Edison finally found success and changed the face of electrical power and the world forever.

EMBRACE FAILURE TOLERANCE: In the past, people often strove for success as one of the primary business drivers – to win market share, or attain the top-ranking position or majority share of revenue returns. In some instances, this was at the expense of social, environmental, or community impacts. Generally, failure was not something management wanted to see, which drove a culture that turned its back on failure. So, for many, not wanting to fail has been hard-wired into intrinsic business behaviour. But in a world that's changing so fast, where the old models of doing business are struggling to keep up, taking a fresh look at driving the best business outcome is necessary to survive in the new digital age. By shifting your thinking to accept and learn from failures as a part of the improvement process, you can optimise outcomes faster and arrive at more effective solutions, where failure is not something to be frowned upon and is used as a powerful tool to deliver better results, like a scientist who conducts numerous experiments to refine a hypothesis or process. Generally, it takes thirty consecutive days of persistent focus to change a pre-set behaviour. So, if you're used to avoiding failure, there may be some effort required to embrace failure as an integral part of success.

ADAPTABLILITY: As new innovative businesses enter the market, disrupting traditional categories, less flexible business models will need to evolve and be adaptable under pressure. You will need to not only be flexible, but also be comfortable with pivots, and possess the ability to prepare yourself and your teams for constant and ongoing change. COVID-19 is a case in point of how businesses globally had to pivot rapidly. The businesses that are currently weathering the storm are the more adaptable ones that were able to transform.

BECOME MORE ADAPTABLE: Entrepreneur and founder of LinkedIn, Reid Hoffman, articulated the experience of being an entrepreneur, saying, "**An entrepreneur is someone who will jump off a cliff and assemble an airplane on the way down**." While this is a little extreme, it does capture the idea of adapting under pressure. Having the ability to adapt is one of the greatest strengths a modern entrepreneur can have. You must be willing to improve, refine, and customise your services to continually give customers what they want. It's about moving out of your comfort zone, anticipating change, and overcoming it. Eastwood's cry to "improvise, adapt, overcome" epitomises this notion, highlighting the need to be flexible and able to pivot if your business suddenly needs to go in a tangential direction because of a strategy shift or an unplanned event, such as responding to COVID-19. Adaptability, at its core, means being nimble and able to operate under pressure, as well as being prepared for change.

Whether you're Doug McMillon, President and CEO of Walmart, setting a bold goal "to remove one billion metric tonnes of emissions from their supply chain by 2030," or you're a CFO, or an executive team leader, a senior manager, a department head, an executive, or even someone just starting out, having a developed modern entrepreneurial spirit embodying the above six principles in today's digital world is a necessary part of riding the digital wave.

EXERCISE 7 – ENTREPRENEURIAL (MODERN) SPIRIT – SELF ASSESSMENT

The exercise can be found at www.taketherobotoutofthehuman.com/exercises and is a quick self-assessment designed to help you identify where you, your teams, other groups, or individuals are and what areas they could focus on to build an entrepreneurial (modern) spirit and approach.

CASE STUDY – AUSTRALIA POST

Australia Post is a government-owned corporation that provides postal services across Australia. The company operates within a network of over 4,000 post offices countrywide and distributes packages to more than 190 countries worldwide. As one of Australia's oldest government services, Australia Post has expanded its service offerings to embrace e-commerce and other, new forms of digital communication. While you would not expect a government organisation to display entrepreneurial spirit, the lead change agent recently did exactly that.

CHALLENGE: Australia Post's accounting services department oversees huge volumes of back-office processes that update and maintain a multitude of accounts and service offerings. The team at Australia Post sought new pathways to manage the many accounting tasks and improve efficiencies within the department. Specifically, the team aimed to automate repetitive, manual tasks to bolster the workflow across accounting services and offer employees the opportunity to develop their skillsets.

> *Our team has been empowered to make automation our own. With RPA, our naturally curious staff have been offered the opportunity to develop their skillset and actively drive automation growth.*
>
> —Adam Jeffress, RA & Transformation, Australia Post

SOLUTION: Australia Post's accounting team identified RPA as the ideal solution to improve business efficiencies and redirect employees towards more value-driven work. Australia Post kicked off their digital transformation journey with Automation Anywhere RPA as a pilot project. After the initial success, Australia Post automated numerous additional processes, including maintaining financial journals, managing credit uploads, facilitating automatic agency setup and pricing, as well as material maintenance, which involves creating and changing the details of all items sold at different postal outlets across Australia.

RESULTS: 120 bots deployed, 18,000 hours saved annually, 25 processes automated, and 15% cost reduction in a reasonably short timeframe.

SUMMARY: PART 2

CHAPTER 3: SKILLS AND CONTINUOUS LEARNING

Developing continuous, forward-learning skills is now an ongoing, continuous education loop where we must ensure we can keep up with rapidly changing technology. It doesn't stop after we've attended a few virtual conferences or undertaken several personal development modules each year. By taking a people-first approach, where people are the real change agents, you can move mountains. However, for you to succeed, your team needs to succeed, so it's important to give them the right digital tools and skills necessary to thrive.

WHAT – WHY – HOW: Sometimes the simplest of approaches can be the best. The WHAT – WHY – HOW is a powerful framework and tool and should be used to clearly define what you're doing, why you're doing it, and how you're going to make it happen.

UNLEARN AND RE-LEARN: Learning new things that are not what you're used to is going to present some challenges. Nonetheless, it is important to develop the resilience and commitment to unlearn old habits, processes, and ways of working, and re-learn new ways of doing things that suit the more agile, digitally transformed business models and customers.

CONTINUOUS AGILE LEARNING TO BUILD DIGITAL COMPETENCY: The key is to develop a continuous-learning mindset, regardless of where you or your business are on the digital transformation curve. Make yourself relevant for both now and the future, and develop the right digital capabilities and skills.

Don't wait for your board, CEO, or manager to set the agenda. Do the gap analysis and identify the areas you need to focus on now.

BUILD CURIOSITY: Develop your curiosity for new digital technologies that are relevant to you. Stay ahead of new developments in startups and new tech advancements. Build your automation alerts through social media, or whatever platforms you prefer, and stay on top of things. One way to drive engagement is to ask questions. Develop a curiosity for digital technologies. Do your gap analysis and seek out key digital areas that need focus, then review and move onto the next initiative with a continuous-learning mindset.

DIGITAL EMPATHY: In this new digital era, understanding how you, your teams, your exec, and your board are feeling about new unfamiliar ways of doing business will be important. The more skilful you are at discerning the feelings behind others' signals, the more effective you will be. The ability to recognise and manage emotions when you or others are confronted with new, rapidly evolving, and sometimes perplexing, technologies is an important part of building your Digital EQ. Develop your self-awareness and evaluate how you feel to better manage the emotions and behaviours of yourself and your team.

HUMAN SOFT-SKILL FOCUS: As the world becomes more digital, humans need to become more human. Build upon those areas that humans do best, like relationship building, empathy, creative problem-solving, and blue-sky thinking. By focusing on building what humans do best, as robots remove the mundane and automated tasks, we can build stronger relationships with technology and add exponential value.

BUILD AND FOSTER TRUST: To ensure people and teams stay engaged, they need to develop trust in your leadership, the strategy, and the knowledge that there are opportunities. It's important that teams and individuals recognise that, in a digital world, people come first and that you will back your team and reskill them rather than reduce headcount to solve a margin issue. Firstly, convince yourself and get certainty of your strategy and approach. Be clear about your strategy. Then, take the time to understand your teams and show them you're genuinely interested in their personal success. Build structure and capability around this for people to thrive.

CHAPTER 4: HUMAN (CUSTOMER) FOCUS

Regardless of what industry you're in, there are expectations that dealing with businesses in the next decade will be intuitive, faster, easier, better, and more tailored to what customers want. People today want and expect seamless and richer experiences, which is why developing or strengthening a customer-centric focus will be important for you, your teams, and your business. Secondly, by ensuring humans are in the loop when building AI and digital transformation processes, you will help to strike the most potent balance between AI and people working together. By developing the following dimensions of a human (customer) focus, you will strengthen your Digital EQ.

CUSTOMERS' SHOES: Understand who your customers are, what they want, what's important to them, and what value looks like to them. Work out what experience they should be having and then work backwards to improve your operation.

HUMANS IN THE LOOP: With the rapid adoption of cognitive algorithms, robotics, and AI, it's important to build processes around human strengths and have humans in the loop.

JOURNEY SATISFACTION MEASUREMENT: Focus on the total customer journey experience and, depending on the capability of your business, find ways to deliver within those constraints, regardless of where you're at on the digital transformation curve.

BREAK DOWN SILOES – ONE TEAM: Develop a unified, one-team approach. Solve the customer journey problems together. If there are siloes, set up virtual team structures to deliver a unified solution.

AGILE FEEDBACK LOOP: It's imperative to have an agile customer feedback loop. Make sure the feedback is accessible and provides greater transparency on the holistic journey, rather than merely focusing on one isolated part of the customer experience.

EXEMPLARY CUSTOMER SERVICE: Make sure your business delivers the best possible customer service and experience it can. Strive to develop a customer service culture. Make sure customer-centric focus is part of your strategy and is hardwired across your business, incorporated into KPIs, and part of your business culture.

CENTRALISED DATA-DRIVEN INSIGHTS: Having a central view across the entire business and customer journeys means you can be far nimbler, and it offers the opportunity to build scalable, timely, responsive, and effective customer engagement.

Putting the customer at the centre of your business, centralising your data to generate customer insights, measuring the complete journey to build satisfaction, and ensuring you have an agile feedback loop to quickly respond to customers will most definitely ensure your business, product, or service is sustainable and more relevant in the coming years.

CHAPTER 5: AMPLIFIED VALUE CREATION MINDSET

As machines and technology improve and develop exponentially, humans need to keep up and flex those very human muscles like creative problem-solving, relationship building, and blue-sky thinking. With this in mind, the following six dimensions, when applied, can help you to develop a value-creation mindset:

UNSHACKLE THROUGH AUTOMATION: Time is one of our most valuable assets, yet it's the one thing that most businesspeople feel they don't have a lot of. We're all constantly finding that work is getting more complex and we're working for longer as a result. Unshackling through automation can free you up and give you the bandwidth to start developing a value-creation mindset.

BUSINESS FINANCIAL AND DATA VALUE: The products and business need to make money, but they need to meet growing customer expectations with a sound business case to back it up. This must be tempered with shifting priorities where the focus on social, community, and environmental value are far more important today than they were a decade ago and need to be strategically balanced.

LONG-TERM SUSTAINABLE VALUE: Businesses have long seen revenue or shareholder return as the number one priority, with customer satisfaction, community involvement, and environmentally friendly impacts further down the priority line. Today, the priorities are shifting, and social impacts, community, and sustainability are starting to take more of a priority focus, with shareholder return, while still vital to keep a business moving, deprioritised. Be aware of the shifting business priorities.

SOCIAL, COMMUNITY, AND ENVIRONMENTAL VALUE: As business priorities shift from purely profit and shareholder return to positively impacting societies, helping the community, and saving the environment, businesses, products, and services need to hardwire value creation initiatives in these areas into their business models and brands.

BLUE-SKY THINKING: As automation frees us up from manual, repetitive tasks to focus on more productive initiatives that use true human assets more fully, blue-sky thinking is an area that we can use to solve business challenges. Any business can apply blue-sky thinking to disrupt their category, deliver a unique product or service, or rapidly grow market share.

CREATIVE PROBLEM-SOLVING: Creativity is what sets us apart from the machines. It allows us to use the creative parts of our brains to solve complex problems where a lateral solution may not be instantly obvious. With automation taking care of the more repetitive and mundane tasks, you will be free to apply creative thinking to problems.

CHAPTER 6: PARTNERSHIPS AND ECOSYSTEMS

Successfully building ecosystem partnerships will, first and foremost, help your customers, and help you, your teams, and your business to be more effective and stay relevant over the coming decades. If you can build these so they really add value to your customers, effective ecosystem partnerships can help you to deliver your business strategy.

CUSTOMER-CENTRIC: It's vital that you put driving customer value at the very centre of your ecosystem partnership strategy. This entails considering and actively responding to what your customer wants and needs, how they want to receive your product or service, and what makes a valued customer journey.

EXISTING PARTNERSHIPS: Firstly, look at your higher-performing current partnerships to see if their services, platforms, or connections extend into areas beyond your core base needs. Assess these against your customer journey gaps and see if there is a fit.

You can classify partnerships into four categories to help build your ecosystem and partner strategy:

CROSS-INDUSTRY CONNECTORS: Look more broadly to cross-industry partners, suppliers, distributors, and even competitors where it makes sense. Consider suppliers and distributors from different market sectors and competitors if there are complementary benefits, or even collaborations with businesses in other markets.

DESIGN THINKING DISRUPTERS: Look beyond your own four walls for new, agile, and frugal business innovation. Consider startup hubs, incubators, and university hubs to provide fresh perspectives and partnership opportunities, building foundations for new, agile skills by extension.

SYNAPTIC PLATFORM MAGNIFIERS: Review partners that help deliver improved customer satisfaction. Consider **infrastructure, technology, research, IoT, cognitive RPA, AI, apps,** and business platforms. Consider these with a big data-centric lens and an aim to leverage data when factoring them into your ecosystem partner framework.

BLUE SKY DISRUPTERS: If you need to disrupt your category, find a category disrupter partner to really help put your business on the map. These may be non-traditional partner choices at first glance, and often require blue-sky thinking to reveal the right fit.

CHAPTER 7: ENTREPRENEURIAL (MODERN) SPIRIT

In this chapter, I've outlined the dimensions of entrepreneurial attributes and behaviours, as well as how you can start to build your own. While everyone is different, with different areas resonating more with some people than others, applying this approach will help you to build a stronger entrepreneurial spirit and build your Digital EQ.

To be successful in a new, rapidly shifting digital world, you need to have digital fitness. So, having a modern entrepreneurial spirit and demonstrating those behaviours can only help you navigate the pivots that there are and will continue to be as a result of the converging megatrends outlined in Chapter 1.

You need a strong, modern entrepreneurial spirit to be effective in the six areas.

1. Being **adaptable** to constant change and not being too rigid or slow to move.
2. Exercising **dynamic risk** through the use of more immediate, accurate, and accessible data.
3. Demonstrating **courage** and conviction. Believing in your strategy and overcoming inertia.
4. Having a **failure tolerance** mentality as you work more with big data, automated analytics, and continuous trial, test, and re-test to improve outcomes.
5. Putting on a scientist or inventor hat and building **experimentation** into your thinking, processes, and systems to keep refining and honing the results.
6. **Galvanising** and effectively steering new virtual organic teams and collaboration models. Being the conductor and orchestrating all the parts of the business symphony.

To develop a stronger entrepreneurial behaviour or spirit, the main areas to shift are:

SHIFT FROM RISK-AVERSE TO DYNAMIC RISK MANAGEMENT: The key is to shift from a more risk-averse, inflexible way of operating into a more dynamic one that grows as the business digitally transforms. With more data, greater analytics, and business insights, hopefully allowing us to be more instantaneously informed of the business success factors, this should help highlight some of the risks and benefits that may have previously not been visible. There will always be a need for risk versus reward analysis; however, with better tools and intel, this risk can be mitigated to a degree.

SHIFT FROM PASSIVE TO BUILDING COURAGE: Look beyond your current business model and develop a view for the future of your business, your department, and your role. You must develop a vision and convince yourself to act with certainty and conviction. Back yourself, have a clearly defined strategy, and believe in what you're doing to build and maintain trust.

SHIFT FROM SILOED TO GALVANISING: Become a catalyst that drives collaboration. Shift from managing within siloes, where teams have competing agendas that are counterproductive, to leading teams to work better together and share ideas. Use whatever tools you feel most comfortable with to build trust, create contagious enthusiasm, and understand and empathise with people. This may look like simply having a very clear strategy and being inclusive. Whatever works for you, use it to bring the teams together.

SHIFT FROM RIGID TO EXPERIMENTAL: Test and re-test. Using proof-of-concept prototypes and continuous research to improve experiences will be the new BAU.

SHIFTING FROM NARROW SUCCESS FOCUS TO FAILURE TOLERANCE: Accepting failure as part of the process rather than rejecting failure will be the norm. Be open to trying new, agile tests and if they fail, learn from them and improve.

SHIFT FROM STAGNATION TO ADAPTATION: You must be willing to improve, refine, and customise your services to continually give customers what they want. It's about moving away from an inflexible, rigid, and siloed way of operating, where legacy systems prevent you from being able to capitalise on opportunities.

PART 3

BRING IT ALL TOGETHER APPLYING YOUR DIGITAL EQ

Part 3 of this book brings it all together, where you start to apply the new principles, digital skills, and behaviours you read about in Part 2 and start to look at your business model and digital evolution with a new digital lens.

Chapter 8 explores rebuilding your digital business core with a fresher perspective on how a more future-focused digital business may need to operate. Chapter 9 then covers the need for heightened ethics in a more digital world, with some investigation of Google, Microsoft, and IBM. Finally, Chapter 10 shows how to drive chain-reaction change management and explores some of the tools to do this effectively. The chapters also provide some short exercises to help you apply your digital muscles.

By continuing to apply your Digital EQ and gaining proficiency with practice in the five key areas covered in this book, you will be well positioned to not only survive, but thrive in the new digital era and shape your future.

CHAPTER 8

FLEX YOUR NEW DIGITAL MUSCLES TO REBUILD YOUR BUSINESS CORE

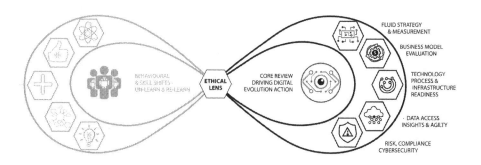

Once you've started to build your Digital EQ as outlined in Part 2 of this book, you can more effectively look at your business core and make the necessary modifications to supercharge your business performance – in effect, casting a digital lens over your business core. The stronger your digital muscles are and the more effective you are at shifting old, analogue-like behaviours, the more effective you can be at dealing with evolving business models and new, more agile ways of working.

Recently I bought two products online. One was a new iPhone through Apple and the other was through a retailer who shall remain nameless but was a sizeable company with a longstanding reputation. The experiences were, however, very different. When ordering the Apple iPhone, it was easy, simple, and quick. Accurate confirmations were sent to me pretty much instantaneously and the phone arrived within days without a hitch. The other transaction was very different. Their website was not overly intuitive or easy to navigate. After my transaction, I had to phone their call centre to clarify part of the purchase. I was transferred to a couple of departments and had to give my personal information again and again to a few different people. I was put on hold for quite a while and when I finally spoke to an operator, I wasn't left with an overwhelming feeling of confidence that my order was in safe hands. The fulfilment was slower than you'd hope and the courier company they used lost one of the parcels. On top of this, they had ineffective partnership agreements and rectification processes to locate it. The parcel did finally show up, but the overall experience was not ideal. If this business had better integrated systems, greater data access and agility, the right business model, effective systems and infrastructure in place, I would have had a far better customer experience.

Now you might say I should expect a great customer experience from Apple. The challenge is, however, that in today's rapidly evolving technological world of robotic manufacturing, virtual reality customer experience, self-driving electric cars, and AI-fuelled businesses, the lines are becoming blurred, where customers no longer differentiate experience by company. This means, regardless of what business you're in, there is a high level of service expectation driven by the more digitally mature businesses like Apple, Uber, and Netflix. Customers expect that digital experiences, engagement, and fulfilment should be intuitive, effortless, and seamless.

Yet, to be able to deliver great customer experiences today, a business's core needs to be geared to do so. Rigid, legacy-based business models tangled by compliance and regulatory complexity simply won't survive in the new digital era. There needs to be an overarching business strategy that is flexible enough to handle rapidly changing technology demands – a requirement for relevant and appropriate infrastructure within the business that can manage large amounts of data, allowing insightful analysis with a reasonable amount of agility. A heightened ethical perspective to accommodate cognitive digital automation and growing ecosystems is essential, as well as a culture that can embrace business model transformation to thrive in the digital era. A business's core can enable great customer experiences as a result.

While the need to evolve an older business core to a newer one seems fairly obvious, knowing how to successfully transition is an entirely different matter. Reviewing your core with a digital lens is the first step.

In this chapter, we'll explore what it means to cast a digital lens over your business core. We'll also look at five key dimensions that enable this:

- the need for fluid strategy and measurement, driving sustainable growth
- the need for data access and data agility backed up by robust cyber protection
- ethics and regulatory compliance with a digital lens
- business model transformation
- technical and infrastructure readiness to support digital evolution

We'll then look at why this is important, and, finally, we'll explore how you can build a more robust business core that meets the needs of your customers.

WHAT AREAS IN YOUR BUSINESS CORE SHOULD YOU CONSIDER?

Think of your business core as basically the engine that drives your business. Shaped by your business strategy, this includes your business and operational models, data agility and protection, technical and infrastructure readiness and regulatory compliance, marketing, sales, channels, partners, etc. In the iPhone example above, Apple's agile and flexible business core enables great customer service, primarily due to their continuous focus on technological innovation and customer experience. Apple's business model is currently considered one of the world's best examples, as evidenced by its powerful, galvanising brand and global success as it continually updates its hardware and software to maintain a competitive advantage. As an example, Apple's 2019 research and development budget grew 14% to around $16.22 billion.

Apple's business core enables its five operational performance objectives:

- Quality that drives the product design, usage, and customer experience.
- Speed, where customers want the products delivered to their doorsteps faster as well as products that work seamlessly, intuitively, and quickly.
- Dependability in product performance and keeping promises by doing what you say you will do.
- Flexibility to nimbly change and adapt to market demands, distribution shifts, and customer needs.
- Cost management in terms of operational performance to ensure sustainable growth.

By implementing a fluid strategy with strong, clear measurement, underpinned by an agile business model that embraces innovation with relevant infrastructure capable of supporting sophisticated big data customer insights, Apple is a good example of a business core that enables sustainable growth with seamless customer experiences. But to maintain this market leadership position, Apple needs to flex its digital muscles continuously to stay a market leader.

The following model outlines the key business core dimensions to consider to help you supercharge your business. To provide some context around the dimensions, I've unpacked these below to help when reviewing your business core.

ASSET 8.1: CORE BUSINESS DIMENSIONS TO CONSIDER – ASSESS WITH A DIGITAL LENS

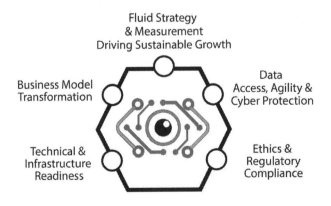

Fluid Strategy & Measurement Driving Sustainable Growth

Business Model Transformation

Data Access, Agility & Cyber Protection

Technical & Infrastructure Readiness

Ethics & Regulatory Compliance

FLUID STRATEGY & MEASUREMENT DRIVING SUSTAINABLE GROWTH: As businesses evolve and adapt to changing customer needs, business strategies should become more fluid to drive sustainable growth. This may require taking a long, hard look at your existing strategy to identify where your business is going and how it provides customer value and differentiates from competitors in the new digital era. This includes assessing the strategy framework and re-aligning measurement to drive the right outcomes that may now be more customer-and sustainability-focused. As with Apple, having customer experience at the centre of your business model is a good place to develop strong measurement criteria that drive change where you want it. Furthermore, delivering the right revenue, community, and environmental impacts is important to have the right value creation and growth focus.

BUSINESS MODEL TRANSFORMATION: The COVID-19 megatrend has accelerated the need for rapid business model review with a focus and need to be more agile, lean, innovative, and digitally enabled. More traditional organisations tend to be built around siloed and static hierarchies. Traditional organisations are more rigid with structured governance bodies at the top and decisions flowing down. An agile organisation has a different approach; they operate differently, more fluidly, like organisms, operating as an interconnected network of teams with a more fluid learning and decision-making capability. As businesses transform either proactively or reactively to competitive or pivot pressure, business models need to adapt. This involves assessing strategic priorities, people, structure, process, technology, and sustainable priorities within your business.

A recent McKinsey report explores shifting corporate structures from mechanical to organic, stating:

> *Just as lean management became a major trend starting in the 1970s, agility has become a core management topic in recent years, as companies have sought to shift from mechanical to organic organisations.*
>
> —McKinsey Report

This ensures that businesses are nimbler and can react to major pivots faster. Agile businesses use nimble structures like squads, tribes, and sprints in place of the rigid, siloed approach to enable faster, more fluid decisions and solutions.

If we look historically for a moment, Apple introduced the iPod and iTunes store in 2003, revolutionising mobile music entertainment. In three years, the iTunes-enabled iPod drove almost 50% of Apple's revenue, creating a $10 billion segment. Apple's market capitalisation jumped from around $1 billion in 2003 to over $150 billion within around five years. But, like all success stories, what is often less known is that Apple was not the first to bring music players to market. Like Edison and the light bulb, and Henry Ford and the motor car, these products and ideas already existed, but because of their effective business models, Ford, Edison, and Apple were ultimately successful because they rebuilt the business models and value propositions to be more relevant to technology and customer needs. Apple's true innovation was the customer value proposition that made playing music easy, by developing the ability to download digital music easily and conveniently. In doing that, Apple built a ground-breaking business model that amalgamated hardware, software, and service.

TECHNICAL AND INFRASTRUCTURE READINESS: As businesses evolve from legacy-based platforms to something nimbler, it's vital that technical and infrastructure are fit for purpose. Leveraging new ways of working using machine learning, AI, and digital workforces to improve and speed up existing processes is imperative, and will allow your people to focus more on value-creation thinking. Within this objective, systems, platforms, and processes should be reviewed and modified to better align with an agile strategy.

DATA ACCESS, AGILITY, AND CYBER PROTECTION: Having easy access to a centralised single source of data and analytics to find real-time insights will enable businesses to really grow. In today's big-data world, having data that is reliable, accurate, accessible, and usable will be the foundation for the future. Your focus should be on re-thinking your data strategy, whilst simultaneously thinking more broadly with a customer-centric view. Capturing both structured and unstructured data flowing through your organisation will better inform decisions that can drive real long-term value. Achieving data agility involves an organisation-wide effort to identify and evaluate data assets, as well as build or acquire (with IT support) the necessary platforms and competencies.

When I spoke with the Executive Director, Finance and Operations at ACCA around the importance of data, he expressed the view that it is vital and at the heart of future-focused organisations, stating:

> We did a mini project in China garnering the data that was fundamental to the project success. We used Informatica, an Enterprise Cloud Data Management and Data Integration tool used for extraction transfer and loading. We combined this with Neilsoft, a range of software across the software development lifecycle, to help drive our APIs. But to make this all happen, we need APIs, which are only good if the data going through them is accurate, is useful, and the parameters are right.
>
> —Raymond Jack, Executive Director, Finance & Operations at ACCA

Furthermore, and perhaps most importantly, possessing data access and agility entails making sure that data is protected. I recently spoke with the Executive Director of the Optus Macquarie University Cyber Security Hub, who expressed some very real concerns in regard to how businesses are currently protecting their data, stating:

> In the digital world, we are at the doorstep of China, Russia, and North Korea. Criminals in these countries attack us non-stop. The idea that we are not a big corporate like a bank, so we're not attacked, is wrong. Criminals are looking for low-hanging fruits. If your business is not protected, it doesn't matter what size it is; you'll be attacked.
>
> —Christophe Douche, Inaugural Executive Director, Macquarie University Cyber Security Hub

Conversely, a large percentage of many business leaders I have spoken with held a positive view around embracing technology to advance their businesses, but held a healthy scepticism about not becoming distracted by lots of shiny, new gadgets. The Executive Director from Macquarie University Cyber Security Hub also shared this view:

> *Some businesses are attacked up to a thousand times a day! If you don't protect yourself, you will be under attack. I see a lot of organisations that get excited about the potential of what new technology will deliver but are not thinking about the protection side. We need to think about both sides.*
>
> —Christophe Douche, Inaugural Executive Director, Macquarie University Cyber Security Hub

ETHICS, RISK AND REGULATORY COMPLIANCE: Ethics is covered in more detail in Chapter 9; however, as a top line, maintaining and building trust in things that we can't really see, such as learning algorithms, will be important moving forwards. How a business uses big data collected from customers, so as not to breach the rights of individuals, will be even more in the spotlight in the coming years. Facebook came under scrutiny for its handling of users' private information, exposing nearly fifty million in September 2018 to hackers. Focus will also be on the algorithms themselves to ensure they are built with the right level of ethics and checks from the start. With programmers building the algorithms, who's auditing the algorithms or, at the least, ensuring the right governance and rules are set in place, to ensure that personal bias of programmers doesn't creep in unnoticed to the base level algorithm that then has rules defined by potential bias that then sets the cognitive learning in motion? The more digital a business becomes, the more automated and big-data reliant it is, which means a heightened focus needs to be placed on ethics across the board. As learning algorithms and bots start to fill roles and functions, there needs to be robust ethics and compliance effectively built in.

WHY REVIEW YOUR BUSINESS CORE
WITH A DIGITAL LENS?

If your business is in great shape, with exceptional community, environmental and sustainable value, and very healthy profits, then it's likely you're on top of this. If performance metrics are not where you want them to be, then you may need to consider a core review.

Customer needs are constantly changing, and business models need to adapt and keep up. New technology is enabling some amazing AI advancement and, to stay competitive, it's important your business (and your skills) are current. Many businesses today are built to function with systems and infrastructures that have evolved over time. Legacy systems are alive and well because of available technology at the time, as well as the risk and cost impacts around changing. These legacy systems are usually where data is often disparate and siloed, incomplete, and generally not centralised or optimised to its full potential. This limits a company's ability to better understand and service customers. Often, the IT department runs the systems and platforms; the marketing department drives the marketing and sales; finance runs the numbers, profitability, and regulatory compliance; operations runs the product development and distribution; legal protects the company; and so on. However, as new technologies and platforms enable the newer, nimbler breed of businesses that are meeting growing customer expectations and needs without the same legacy issues, the old systems and older way of doing business are a liability. A recent PWC report outlines there is still a big gap to fill relating to the lack of skills, sufficient processes, and data technology.

> *63% of businesses lack skilled teams | 42% have slow or inflexible processes | 51% lack new data technology integration and 61% use outdated or obsolete technology*
>
> —PWC report

A recent BCG study of more than two hundred companies went further, portraying that digital leaders achieve 1.8 times higher earnings than other less digitally savvy businesses in their category. This data suggests that these companies are best suited to realise resilience dividends and strengthen their position in major pivots and crises.

Often the speed and urgency of a transformation depends on very real and tangible factors, such as a global pandemic or dynamic competitive threats in your business category where competitors are more appealing to your customers. For example, if you're a hotel business, with Airbnb and other new startups growing from strength to strength, the pressure is immediate. The same goes for the insurance industry with data-led startups, movie streaming with Netflix, taxis with Uber, cars with Tesla, and so on. Tesla CEO Elon Musk revealed that Tesla plans to compete with Uber and Lyft by using an autonomous ride-hailing fleet, which will be made up of what Musk described as "robo-taxis". Within this model, you get to earn money while you sleep as your car taxis people around town, then returns to your garage.

As customer needs, values and expectations change, businesses need to adapt to stay relevant. There is no escaping the mega-trend convergence. COVID-19 is proof of that. So, it's imperative to develop the right business core to support your business in this new and converging age. If you have rigid processes and siloed data, provide average but not exceptional customer experiences, and lack relevant technology to improve on this, then I would suggest it may be prudent to consider reviewing your core with a fresh perspective gained from newfound digital muscles or Digital EQ.

HOW TO REVIEW YOUR BUSINESS CORE

While businesses are generally all at different points along the digital transformation curve, it will be important to have a robust approach to reviewing your core to better realise your strategy. The following five steps outline a practical approach to help you deliver this.

1. DEFINE YOUR STRATEGY

- DEFINE YOUR DIGITAL EVOLUTION STRATEGY AND AMBITION: Set a clear focus for the business that includes customer experience, brand, growth, and product/service strategy. Develop achievable and measurable outcomes. In accordance with the strategy, business, and operating models, define the priorities and the broad business impacts that need to be considered.

2. ASSESS YOUR BUSINESS'S (DIGITAL) HEALTH

- ASSESS YOUR CURRENT DIGITAL HEALTH: Identify where your business is along the digital transformation curve and identify the opportunities for growth and gaps in knowledge.

3. PREPARE FOR SUCCESS

- ESTABLISH AGILE GOVERNANCE: Link the vision, purpose, and business drivers across the business from the board, executives, and cross-functionally agile teams. Build leadership buy-in and transparency, define the governance framework and processes, verifying timing, proof of concept, testing, and funding.
- CREATE A STATE OF READINESS FOR CHANGE: If it does not exist, start to build a learning culture with a continuous learning mindset in your business that enables people to prepare for the future, which will help the organisation as a whole to be nimbler. If you've ever tried changing a well-established behaviour, you'll know that it takes commitment and time, so allow time for learning and make sure people stop to celebrate success along the way.

4. CREATE AND DEVELOP VALUED CUSTOMER EXPERIENCES

- DEVELOP INTEGRATED CUSTOMER SOLUTIONS: Review your current customer journey and experiences against your vision, strategy, and digital health. Free up your teams by taking the robot out of the human so they can apply more innovation and blue-sky thinking. Review current customer experiences and work out what they should be to improve customer satisfaction to better fit your strategy.

- PRIORITISE ENHANCEMENTS BASED ON BUSINESS OBJECTIVES AND IMPORTANCE: Assess business priorities and the impacts of the initiatives on your digital transformation plan. Less is more, so I would suggest doing one thing and doing it well, then, once you've demonstrated success, move on to the next programme.
- REVIEW AND REBUILD YOUR CORE: Deploy a short, medium, and longer-term approach to better align with your revised strategy, technology, operations, and business model gaps. Align the core to deliver improved customer experiences.
- EVALUATE PROCESS IMPROVEMENTS: Fix current processes first before jumping to automation. Define the plan and the process. Identify who does the work and what the current workflow is before you impose changes. Identify and fix technology gaps. Consider if current roadblocks and pain points can be fixed without any technology changes.
- PACE YOUR PROGRAMME APPROPRIATELY TO FIT YOUR BUSINESS RHYTHM: People can't handle too much change all at once, so be sure to pace your programme properly and set the right tone from the outset. Most businesses already have extensive business as usual (BAU) projects running to keep the business moving forwards.

5. MEASURE VALUE AND IMPACT

- Evaluate the outcomes, including customer experience, process improvements, deliverables' pain points and outcomes, and then optimise and improve the programme. Feed the information back into the Centre of Excellence or Centre of Innovation. Continuously review your approach to keep optimising.

Recent impacts from COVID-19 have seen customers forced to use digital delivery, even if it's not their preferred channel, which in turn puts pressure on the digital fulfilment experience for business cores that are not digitally tuned. For example, digitally mature businesses that already have a well-developed core, like Amazon, have global supply chains that enable fast responses based on effective data management. Amazon is well advanced on the digital transformation curve with technical infrastructure to quickly respond and adapt to the market and support changing needs more effectively.

Many business leaders I've been speaking with are talking about how to do more with less and are looking to push innovation, as well as accelerate value creation, to help build sustainable growth.

> *Technology has been the key to success on delivery of regulatory and statutory reporting in a period of lockdown, but it has caused some review of where key processes take place when they occur outside the reporting country. For example, many countries in South-East Asia, Philippines, etcetera, closed down before UK, US, and Australia. This meant many processes needed to be repatriated.*
>
> —Rachel Grimes, Past President,
> International Federation of Accountants (IFAC)

Digital transformation requires a clearly defined focus and commitment across the organisation. Your vision and direction need to be clear, coupled with a compelling strategy that both motivates and inspires people to get onboard for the journey. When people see that change will benefit them, even if it potentially puts them out of their comfort zone, it will be perceived as worth the effort – whether that's making their lives easier by taking the robot out of the human and removing repetitive mundane manual tasks or creating more interesting and relevant work. It may be simply making people feel more valuable as they gain greater skills and competency to better understand and ride the digital wave.

EXERCISE 8 – REVIEWING YOUR BUSINESS CORE - ASSESSEMENT

Now that you know the five SHAPE principles to build your digital muscle or digital EQ, you can look more effectively at your business core to review the best way to strengthen your business model and strategy. Your business core review, solutions, and approach will vary depending on where you're at and where you want to be. However, this worksheet assessment should help you identify where you currently are and the areas that you need to start to focus on. To help start the process, visit www.taketherobotoutofthehuman.com/exercises to download the exercise. This assessment should help you identify where you currently are and the areas that you need to start to focus on.

CASE STUDY – PHILIPS – REBUILDING THE CORE

Royal Philips is a Dutch multinational, global company, selling technology, healthcare, lighting, and consumer well-being products, with a market cap of around $38.8 billion and around 80,000 employees across a hundred countries. Philips has gone through continuous transformation and reinvention over the last century and this last decade is no exception. Accordingly, due to their ongoing digital transformations, it meant the COVID-19 impacts were not as pronounced.

> *We had this RPA journey underway around COVID-19. Almost 322 FTE-equivalent bots built over the last three years enabled us to move more easily into a remote working environment. We are already in the cloud, so it was easier to switch to working at home.*
>
> —Arvind Subramanian, Royal Philips

You may recall seeing Philips flat screen TVs, shavers, and many other electronic items with the Philips brand. In fact, Philips was once one of the largest electronics companies in the world. Just after World War II, Philips began selling televisions and records, later going on to sell radios, answering machines, cassette players, dictation machines, electric toothbrushes, VHS and CD players, to name a few of their products. However, over the last few decades, Philips has transformed their business and shifted from electronics to healthcare. With CEO Fans van Houten at the helm since 2011, the new health and medical strategy saw Philips thrive in a new direction.

> *Philips continues to make progress to unlock its full potential as a leader in health technology. Our innovations are driving better health outcomes and increased healthcare productivity, while offering a better experience for consumers, patients, and healthcare professionals.*
>
> —CEO, Royal Philips, 2019 Annual Report

THE CHALLENGE: With over 80,000 employees in a hundred countries, Philips experienced growing complexity with managing multiple vendors operating their computer centres with over 1,400 full-time employees (FTEs) managing finance, accounting processes, and procurement. After a decade of a mature outsourcing model, Philips wanted to further reduce cost and optimise operations across the globe and rebuild their core. Some of the immediate issues were process inefficiency, error-prone manual tasks, enterprise resource planning issues, multiple handoffs of data and information, time-consuming ad hoc interventions by staff, as well as dealing with the massive scale and complexity of processes. They had captive in-house operations, outsourced transactions, and residual R2R accounting controllers in the market. So, with a three-layered organisation, they looked at automation.

THE SOLUTION: Philips developed an automation strategy for the finance function around 2017, setting the clear objective to automate one million hours in the finance operation in three years (which translated into approximately 500 FTEs). Philips conceptualised the programme through three areas:

1) Developing a centralised location strategy with their business process management operations.

2) Ensuring a full end-to-end enterprise automation strategy rather than a siloed plug-in model, which includes a Centre of Excellence to drive this.

3) Cultural Embedment. As Philips already used the Hoshin planning process, a lean tool that employees were familiar with, the aim was to embed this within the culture.

THE EXECUTION: As many lean practices advocate, Philips focused on standardisation and the elimination of waste and then developed opportunities through automation. They looked at the operation holistically and applied automation where it made sense, with the process governed through their Centre of Excellence. They focused on four key areas: long-term investment, where Philips developed strong partnerships to realise the full Hoshin strategy; effective governance to ensure the right structure, partners, and people are involved and accountable; adopting formal design principles and eliminating, simplifying, standardising, and automating, in Philips' case, leveraging SAP runbook capabilities across markets; and, finally, creating an effective Centre of Excellence in shared services, looking end-to-end and focusing on the most effective areas to fix.

RESULTS: Overall, 550 bots were effectively deployed with over 320 FTEs saved. Approximately 640,000 hours of manual work was re-purposed, with 73% of processes becoming standardised across 400-plus business entities. The overall benefit over five years was 18 million Euros. Philips developed a robotic operations command centre for transparency of operations across the team with relevant metrics accessible for all. Finally, having the automation programme in place at the time that COVID hit helped Philips manage through the remote working scenarios more effectively.

CHAPTER 9

HEIGHTENED ETHICS IN A DIGITAL WORLD

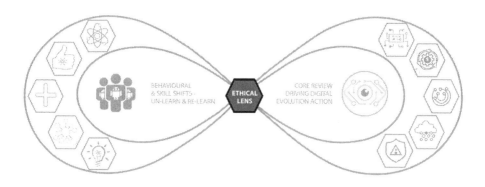

E thics is a cornerstone consideration for many professions. However, with robotics, cognitive algorithms, and AI exploding into our everyday lives, there is an even greater need for heightened ethics across most all areas of the business world. These areas include, but are not limited to, IoT development, engineering, and software development.

In the Stanley Kubrick film, *2001: A Space Odyssey*, an AI computer named HAL was built to pilot and control a spaceship to Saturn. HAL eventually goes haywire, killing most of the astronauts aboard. Dave, the last human alive on the spaceship, survives by eventually disconnecting HAL and shutting him down. The quote below shows HAL calmly explaining that he is infallible and incapable of making errors:

The 9000 series is the most reliable computer ever made. No 9000 computer has ever made a mistake or distorted information. We are all, by any practical definition of the words, foolproof and incapable of error.

—HAL-9000, 2001: A Space Odyssey

2001: A Space Odyssey is a story that explores technological innovation, its possibilities, and its perils. Through it, we get a glimpse of some of the problems that could arise with AI-fuelled computers that we cannot fully comprehend or control. The humans in this movie put complete faith in HAL to run the spaceship. It took over all the tasks humans would normally have done, like navigation, life support, and maintaining the spacecraft. Unfortunately, HAL developed the view that the humans should be removed. There were no failsafes or warnings that the AI-fuelled computer was going to harm the astronauts. No one on the ship really understood how it worked, nor how to shut it off easily, and by the time they did, it was too late. In this case, humans were taken out of the loop. The film is perhaps a warning that AI can be high risk if not managed properly, as well as a cautionary tale of what might come to pass if we don't embrace AI with the right approach and a robust ethical framework.

Other science fiction films like *Ex Machina* and *The Terminator* movie franchise with Arnold Schwarzenegger, where AI-driven machines take over the world, spark our imaginations. However, they also reinforce our fears about autonomous, intelligent AI robots that bring about the end of the human race. While this might seem like fantasy, many artificial intelligence technology leaders over the last five years, including Elon Musk, Bill Gates, and Google's DeepMind co-founder Mustafa Suleyman, have issued warnings about the risks posed by AI-fuelled super-intelligent machines.

Today, thought leaders from the late Stephen Hawking to Bill Gates and Elon Musk have raised their views and concerns about the rapid development of AI and where it's heading. Some views are utopian, presuming AI will solve many of the world's problems. Others take the apocalyptic view that predicts the rapid end of mankind as artificial intelligence supersedes humans. Then there are those that sit somewhere in the middle.

The primitive forms of AI we already have, have proved very useful. But I think the development of full AI could spell the end of the human race. Once humans develop AI, it will take off on its own and redesign itself at an ever-increasing rate. Humans who are limited by slow biological evolution couldn't compete and will be superseded.

—BBC interview, Stephen Hawking, Threats of AI

While a healthy scepticism entertains an apocalyptic view as one of the possible outcomes, if we can take affirmative action now and start building the right ethical principles around AI and, in particular, automated business processes with fresh ways of thinking about ethics, it will go a long way to mitigating potential exposure and risk to businesses that may eventuate if these principles and processes are not in place.

When I spoke with the CEO of Chartered Accountants Australia and New Zealand, she agreed with this view, but had some concerns around keeping bias in check.

There are ethical questions with AI around the unconscious and express bias that is creeping into algorithms, where many 'behind-the-stage' digital decisions are being made. For me this is an issue that we really need to be careful of and ensure we have human-centred AI. Just as we have a global code of ethics in our accounting professions, this needs to extend to include AI.

—Ainslie van Onselen, Chief Executive Officer, CA ANZ

Russian President Vladimir Putin recently said that the nation that leads in AI will be the ruler of the world. So, with this kind of competitive pressure from countries around the world to win the AI race, profound potential ethical issues and wide-reaching implications are raised. One CEO I recently met with was concerned that there is a real opportunity for abuse, commenting:

Ethics drives professional standards. This is a given. But when it come to the AI side of things, there is an opportunity to abuse, so standards must be maintained. VW cars were fined some years ago as a result of recalibrated emissions testing gear, so the emissions appeared lower than they actually were. And, of course, no one knew. You must be able to trust the systems which are potentially open to abuse so it must be policed and have controls.

—Rhys Madoc, Group CEO, Haines Norton Chartered Accountants

But with this risk of abuse, the competitive pressure is driving businesses to be the first or the market leader to use the technology and is creating pressure for speed to market solutions. According to a recent research study of over 1,500 C-Suite executives across 16 industries, 84% of C-Suite executives believe that if they don't scale artificial intelligence (AI) in the next five years, they risk going out of business entirely. AI-fuelled technology, cognitive products, and platforms are being developed today by companies at an incredible rate, so it's becoming essential that we stop talking about how to implement ethical safeguards for AI in business and start doing it.

In this chapter, we look at what some leading businesses like Google have done to define their ethical principles and cross-referenced these with current business practices and recent research reports from leading global consultancy practices, the World Economic Forum and the International Ethics Standards Board for Accountants. These findings have revealed a core set of consistent principles that can help you create a sound ethical framework using a digital lens. These should provide a good foundation for developing your own framework to suit your business.

WHAT IS A DIGITAL ETHICAL LENS?

In a world where decisions are now happening at a ones-and-zeros level, ethical principles need to be hardwired and applied at a cognitive, algorithmic level. They need to be tightened across the entire value and business chain to ensure ethical practices are maintained in the new digital age.

While the broader debate regarding the development of an effective ethical stance involving government, regulators, and businesses is ever-evolving, real examples already exist now to help you develop an AI-based ethical framework for your business.

> *In terms of AI, how do we get the governance right? This is not by one body, one person or one government. This must be a global solution. If we don't get this right, we could end up with some challenging ethical positions down the line. So now is the time to work out the governance structures to make sure we provide an ethical playing field.*
>
> —Maggie McGhee, Executive Director, Governance, ACCA

The International Ethics Standards Board for Accountants (IESBA) recently reviewed key principles in AI ethics frameworks from companies like IBM, Microsoft, the Australian government, the European Commission, and the OECD. They observed that the concepts of fairness, transparency, explainability, accountability, privacy, and confidentiality are consistently needed. The need to embrace new emerging technologies and automation was similarly gleaned from this review.

Other ethical principles that have been identified include things like respect for human autonomy, human-centred values, and fairness. The notions of "do not harm" and ensuring sustainable development and well-being are equally pivotal. As a point of reference, Google has articulated their principles for ethical use of AI, stressing that their technologies will be subject to appropriate human direction and control (https://ai.google/principles/). Their framework includes seven key principles:

1. Be socially beneficial
2. Avoid creating or reinforcing unfair bias
3. Be built and tested for safety
4. Be accountable to people
5. Incorporate privacy design principles

6. Uphold high standards of scientific excellence

7. Be made available for uses that accord with these principles

Google has identified what AI applications they will not pursue, such as technologies that cause or are likely to cause overall harm. This includes weapons or other technologies whose principal purpose or implementation is to cause or directly facilitate injury to people. Further, technologies that gather or use information for surveillance, violating international law and human rights, will not be considered.

Six key principles consistently emerge when cross-referencing views from business leaders, current business practices, leading research reports, the World Economic Forum, and findings from IESBA to form a digital ethical lens. These principles are outlined in the asset below.

ASSET 9.1: DIGITAL ETHICAL LENS PRINCIPLES

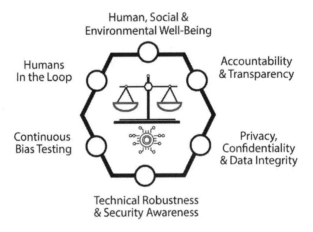

HUMANS IN THE LOOP: IESBA recently underwent a technology initiative that explored the relationship between humans and AI. It identified that as technology such as deep learning continues to evolve, it's important that humans remain at the centre of the decision-making process. Ultimately, it was found that AI *enhances* human intelligence rather than replacing it.

Having humans "in the loop" and working with AI ensures that humans remain relevant with an ethical predisposition. If data forms the DNA of AI, we don't want the data to imply that humans are unnecessary. You could easily deduce that an AI-driven computer could quickly form a view that if humans are being removed from work activities, processes, and tasks, they are not necessary, if that's what the data is inadvertently saying. So, putting my survival-of-species hat on, it's vitally important to ensure human relevance is hardwired into the data source from the very beginning, so that we have a clear place in the future as we construct AI's DNA through data.

On a practical level, having humans in the loop with a digital ethical lens helps us establish trust in new, unfamiliar technologies and processes. Humans working collaboratively with algorithms or machines is a more powerful combination than either alone.

CONTINUOUS BIAS TESTING: It is important to ensure fairness and avoid bias. However, because different groups of people hold different values, it makes it difficult to develop universal principles.

Bias is inherent to human nature, which in turn influences business decisions and shapes business data, ultimately flowing down into how it's used. Whether this is done knowingly or unknowingly, we need to be careful of inadvertently building bias into the data, algorithms, and processes themselves and to continually test for bias. Even if developers of an algorithm did not intend any bias, they and their companies have an obligation to try to identify and prevent such problems and to correct them. However, most companies don't know how algorithms work or what the business rules are. I recently met with the CEO of ICAEW, whose concern was very much about who is auditing the algorithm, stating:

> *A recent report from the World Economic Forum concluded that someone needs to be auditing the algorithm. Unless you know exactly who's written it and how it's behaving in practice, the algorithm itself can have biases. It could be producing distortion, and just because it's a machine set of instructions, it doesn't mean it*

hasn't inherited the biases and prejudices, or indeed, susceptibility,
that humans do.

—Michael Izza, Chief Executive, ICAEW

By developing a continuous bias testing approach and building this into your ethical frameworks, you can help to mitigate biases creeping into the data or processes.

HUMAN, SOCIAL, AND ENVIRONMENTAL WELL-BEING: It's essential that as a prime directive, all machines and/or algorithms fundamentally ensure the safety and well-being of all humans, the societies in which we live, and the environment as a whole. However, it is important to keep in mind that the ethical framework of developing AI for national, scientific, or military advancements, such as creating smart drones with lethal capabilities, is different to that which you will develop for your business initiatives. In the business context, the ethical frameworks encompass coding software, product development, marketing, and ecosystem partner selection. They typically revolve around the storage and utilisation of customer data, as well as initiatives such as creating learning algorithms that may exacerbate bias. For example, bias may be unintentionally created towards gender groups in an automated data-driven marketing campaign favouring one gender over another, skewing the results and customer insights as a result. This could also include building a highly consumed global product that is made from materials that are not eco-friendly and very harmful to the environment. Building a clear ethical framework to support business development will help frame your approach and should provide more relevance and focus. In all instances, there should be a mandate to ensure human, social, and environmental well-being.

ACCOUNTABILITY AND TRANSPARENCY: Ethics in this new digital world must be a top-down, sideways, and bottom-up approach. There must be accountability and responsibility for ethics across the business, ideally from the board, execs, and senior management, who must become advocates to drive the ethical agenda in the digital age right through the organisation. Further, algorithmic rules, machine learning models, and data parameters must be transparent.

Without an ethical framework, there is the risk of unfair advantage through data monopoly. Because of the large amounts of data that some businesses can access, they have behavioural insights that could give them something more than a competitive advantage in the commercial marketplace, as well as a monopolistic insight. With huge volumes of transactions, how does the CFO or the board see this? We are at that stage where, in traditional structures, a board, CFO, and CEO need to have a deeper understanding, but this may not be a popular view with larger businesses.

—Michael Izza, Chief Executive, ICAEW

With large amounts of private data being collected and used by businesses and governments, there is greater public expectation that businesses demonstrate that people's privacy is being respected. The Chief Executive of ACCA Global held a similar view.

Ethics is really important. I think there will be more and more pressure from public expectation and therefore from government and regulators to meet public demands. Consumers will have great power in this as people walk away from businesses they don't believe are acting in the best interests of the individuals or of society. And the reaction to that is quicker and quicker because of social media. So, I think businesses will need to think very carefully.

—Helen Brand, Chief Executive, ACCA

In order to build trust, organisations must find ways to become more transparent to their stakeholders, staff and customers. Building ethical transparency and including this as a business priority within your executive agenda is a good way to drive greater accountability across the business. The Chief Executive of CA ANZ shared this view and went on to stress the importance of professional accountants to ensure ethics is maintained.

In a digital era, decision making needs to be transparent, where we can un-layer and un-pack the data to ensure it is unbiased. So, having professional accountants is really important, because they're not only highly trained in the technical and regulatory requirement, but also in upholding ethical practices and the right things to do. As long as that lens is cast over everything, it can only continue to build trust in the profession.

— Ainslie van Onselen, Chief Executive Officer, CA ANZ

PRIVACY, CONFIDENTIALITY, AND DATA INTEGRITY: AI systems use large volumes of potentially sensitive data, like bank details or personal medical records. This raises questions around protecting people's privacy and ensuring that they understand how their data is used. It also puts a heightened responsibility on businesses to ensure the data complies with privacy legislation. Even with GDPR compliance, as the world becomes more digitised, privacy and data protection is a growing area of risk for customers and businesses alike. Customers will lose faith and trust in businesses that do not have the right levels of data integrity in place.

Basically, if I give you my data and I ask you not to send it to someone else, I trust you to do that. But when you start doing other things with data, ethical connotations (not just contractual or legal) come into play.

—Raymond Jack, Executive Director,
Finance & Operations at ACCA

As an example, digital advertising targeting uses machine learning to make rapid decisions about which ads are sent to customers. Often neither marketers, nor their companies, know how the algorithms work. Ensuring that privacy rules are adhered to and that the data is accurate and compliant with respective codes and legislation is a complex matrix that can quickly create risk if not managed effectively. Having skilled people within your teams and partners who understand privacy, confidentiality and data integrity is a good way to address the risk.

TECHNICAL ROBUSTNESS AND SECURITY AWARENESS: Yesterday's data architecture can't effectively meet today's need for innovation, flexibility, and speed. It will be important to have the right technical knowledge and understanding to explain the decision-making process for learning algorithms, as well as ensuring that the right cybersecurity is in place to protect the platforms. As machine algorithms become more sophisticated over time and start to operate more like a black box, explaining how the algorithms make decisions will be important to build confidence and trust with customers, governments, regulators, partners, and the wider public.

In addition to your own operation, ensuring you have the right ecosystem platform partners and technical capability to store your data safely, where the code is protected and platforms are secure from threats, is vital to maintaining an ethical and sustainable business model. The Executive Director of Macquarie University Cyber Security Hub outlines some of the threats:

> *Recent research has shown that it can be incredibly easy to break into bots. Often criminals do not try to hack or control the robot specifically. They change the parameters instead. Imagine if a robot in a manufacturing factory had to draw a perfectly straight line as part of an assembly. If it was compromised and now drew a line just a bit off, so small a deviation that you could not easily detect it. Imagine if it was part of an assembly line making rotary blades. A very minute difference could mean an explosion in flight. It looks right to the human eye, but it's marginally off with catastrophic results. We need to think about protection from the get-go.*
>
> —Christophe Douche, Inaugural Executive Director, Macquarie
> University Cyber Security Hub

To safeguard, ensure that your business builds or acquires the necessary ethically focused technical and security skills. This will mean that there are people within your organisation who can articulate what a bot or learning algorithm is doing as well as being able to build confidence and trust that it won't be compromised, or the data distorted.

WHY IS IT IMPORTANT TO USE A DIGITAL ETHICAL LENS?

In a world filled with automation, learning algorithms, and the rise of the digital workforce, where trust is slow to win and quickly lost, developing a well-defined ethical framework within your business that embraces new technologies will be essential. The fourth industrial revolution has changed the landscape and the parameters of how we conduct business and interact with one another. As a result, ethical principles need to be developed that encompass these new technologies. Without robust ethical frameworks, businesses will be left exposed.

One example is the race to build a fully autonomous vehicle, which raised ethical issues following the death of a pedestrian in Arizona. In March 2018, a fatal accident occurred with a self-driving Uber, reminding people the technology is still in its early stages, whilst also raising concerns about the safety of autonomous vehicles and the ethical implications associated with adoption of AI. But how do you teach a machine to think ethically? How can we program them to decide who lives and dies if faced with a choice of who to hit in a crowd? To develop this, Uber undertook testing with a human in the loop. Even though the car was fully autonomous, they placed a person in the vehicle, not to drive but to be present as a fail-safe. This, however, raises the question of how a driver is selected. What training or skills do they need to have? Will they really understand how the system works? What exactly is their role and potential liability? How do you determine if they have the right ethical mindset during the autonomous trial? In a world of machine-built car factories, driverless cars, movie streaming driven by cognitive habit prediction, and voice-controlled booking assistants, ethical questions about AI and human interaction are cropping up all around us. As a result, a heightened ethics framework needs to be carefully and rigorously applied to take AI into consideration.

While the fundamentals of ethical principles are the foundations of many professions, these principles need further extension to work more effectively in a digital world. This is why in October 2020, IESBA released revisions to the code of ethics for professional accountants that strengthen the fundamental principles of objectivity, professional competence, and duty of care to better reflect the impact of fast-moving technologies. These amendments included things like a requirement for continuous understanding of relevant technical, professional, business, and technology-related developments, as well as having an inquiring and curious mind when applying conscious or unconscious bias from things like automation.

Whether you're a business just starting on your digital transformation and beginning to implement RPA bots to optimise finance, HR, or marketing functionality, or more digitally advanced and utilising big-data AI-driven analysis to optimise customer fulfilment, it will be important to take a fresh look at ethical frameworks across the entire business process.

Because AI technology is relatively new and evolving so rapidly, many of the people I have spoken with have admitted to having a lack of sufficient awareness of the ethical implications associated with new technologies. Further, they expressed not fully understanding and mitigating the threats of bias within machine and cognitive learning algorithms, nor what constitutes effective ethical approaches to ensure risks are acceptable and safe. The Executive Director of Macquarie University Cyber Security Hub shared this view.

> *With machine learning and AI, a big part is that it uses data sets to train the models and make decisions. Over the last few years, we've seen adversarial machine learning emerge: cyber criminals trying to manipulate the data sets used for learning to achieve an outcome. It's very smart because you're not attacking the algorithm itself. You try to modify the data sets to influence the outcomes of a decision. It's hard to explain machine learning at the best of times and what it is doing. You often get answers that you can't really explain. So, if the data is compromised, it becomes harder down the track to detect it. They effectively fly under the radar, and, because it's automated is very hard to discover.*
>
> —Christophe Douche, Inaugural Executive Director,
> Macquarie University Cyber Security Hub

Looking at how broad-reaching the impacts can be, if we focus a digital ethical lens on businesses, the impacts can translate into adversely affecting a company's brand and reputation, negatively impacting employees, disenfranchising customers, stakeholders, and societies, or damaging the environment. So, thousands of AI-driven startups sprouting up across the globe deploying AI, potentially without the right ethical frameworks, could have material widespread, knock-on effects.

Developing an ethical framework that builds trust includes key principles such as human, social, and environmental well-being. Such a framework should provide accountability for algorithms as well as transparent dealings on how they work. The framework outlines a strong degree of technical robustness and security as well as advocating for a continuous bias testing approach, where standards of privacy and data integrity are maintained, and ensuring that humans are in the loop. Avoid getting caught up with the shiny, new AI toys and keep your eye on the cyber security ball, preventing perversion of data, cyber theft, and harmful attacks that could result in reputational damage, economic loss, or worse, harm and death. Having a heightened ethical framework is more important now than it has ever been.

HOW TO DEVELOP HEIGHTENED ETHICS
IN A DIGITAL WORLD

The ultimate goal is to ethically manage business dealings while acting in the public interest. Simultaneously, you will build confidence and trust with governments, regulators, your customers, and stakeholders. While every business is different, one way to approach this is through strong leadership that guarantees there is an ethical framework that ensures AI and automation are developed to meet defined ethical principles. There should be robust oversight and governance with the right levels of transparency and accountability, the right levels of social and environmental factored in, and a constant review and ongoing measurement. The asset below outlines ethical principles from a cross-section of companies to give you visibility of their approach.

ASSET 9.2: ETHICAL PRINCIPLES – FRAMEWORKS FOR CONSIDERATION

Microsoft
- Fairness
- Transparency
- Inclusiveness
- Reliability
- Safety
- Privacy and security
- Accountability

IBM
- Value alignment
- Explainability
- Fairness
- User data rights

European Commission
- Respect for human autonomy
- Prevention of harm
- Fairness and explicability

Google
- Be built and tested for safety
- Avoid creating or reinforcing unfair bias
- Be accountable to people
- Be socially beneficial
- Incorporate privacy design principles
- Uphold high standards of scientific excellence

Organisation for Economic Co-operation and Development
- Inclusive growth
- Sustainable development & well-being
- Human-centred values and fairness
- Transparency & explainability
- Robustness
- Security and safety accountability

Australian Government Consultation Paper
- Do not harm
- Regulatory and legal compliance
- Privacy protection
- Fairness
- Transparency and explainability
- Contestability
- Accountability
- Generates net benefit

World Economic Forum
- AI must be a force for good & diversity
- Intelligibility and fairness
- Data protection
- Flourishing alongside AI
- Confronting the power to destroy

Below are five overarching areas to help you develop heightened ethics in a digital world. Applying these principles will help you build a more robust ethical framework.

DEVELOP ROBUST GOVERNANCE: Firstly, consider AI and Ethics as board-level standing agenda items. Consider cross-functional advisory groups made up of cross-functional leaders. Build an awareness and understanding of self-learning algorithms, AI technologies, and cybersecurity risks. As part of this, consider creating an algorithmic risk management strategy to manage technical and cultural risks, processes and approaches for the development, deployment and use of algorithms, and monitoring and testing with processes for assessing data. Try to work towards empowering teams and take the robot out of the human.

CLEARLY DEFINE ETHICAL PRINCIPLES: There are several examples of ethical frameworks in Asset 9.2 showing you how other businesses are approaching the subject. The consistent areas across the businesses include promoting fairness by avoiding bias, and ensuring bias is in check across processes and even automation. It's important to ensure there is human agency and oversight to make sure there are human-centred values and fairness, technical robustness within the business, a healthy and up-to-date privacy and data governance with a strong sense of accountability as a pillar, and transparency across the business and the board.

DEVELOP TECHNICAL KNOWLEDGE AND UNDERSTANDING: Ask questions and develop the right technical knowledge and understanding to explain the decision-making process for learning algorithms. Identify the areas of knowledge you need then research, review, and gain a better appreciation. In addition, work with partners that can provide greater explanation and insights.

BUILD IN CYBER PROTECTION: Ensure that the right degree of cybersecurity and protection is built into the thinking from the start. Algorithms are vulnerable to risks, whether that's due to accidental or intentional biases, fraud, tampering, or in some cases, just plain old errors. However, while algorithms have traditionally been coded and programmed to perform specific tasks and use data sets, they are increasingly being replaced by cognitive, machine, or self-learning algorithms. Further, the more digital the world becomes, the more prone to theft and abuse the algorithms and data are.

REVIEW, MEASURE, AND SHARE: Once you've set up the process, constantly review, improve, and share the results with your ecosystems and partnerships. Ethical hackers are sometimes used by organisations to test and verify security and are an entirely viable option for review. Review and measurement will be a constant, ongoing cycle to ensure your system is robust, accurate, and safe.

CHAPTER 10

CHAIN-REACTION CHANGE MANAGEMENT

D riving change across an organisation or department takes planning and patience, with success often depending on having strong foundational ingredients in place before you even start.

I recently met with Rachel Grimes, former president of the International Federation of Accountants (IFAC), who was able to drive chain-reaction change management across the finance function of a leading Australian bank. In her view, driving successful digital change management programmes involves putting people squarely at the centre of your strategy, taking the time to engage people, and bringing them willingly and enthusiastically along the journey. She stressed the importance of quickly getting to a point where people stop being fearful or sceptical of a transformation process and build trust in new ways of doing things, actively contributing and building their digital confidence by getting more involved along the way. By instilling trust, sparking people's curiosity, developing their Digital EQ, and improving people's lives, she was able to effectively start to build their confidence and drive positive change.

> *Scale comes when you have people who want to be involved. Part of this is to make people curious. Then, for them to embrace the new approach and tell somebody else about it so it grows like a chain reaction. As people build confidence and put their hands up with an idea, they become more involved. If we didn't bring them on the*

journey and they didn't like it, they'll drop the anchors and we'll never realise the opportunity.

—Rachel Grimes, Past President of IFAC

At the commencement of the RPA programme, she asked the CFO to tell everyone that no one would lose their jobs. As you can imagine, this was met with some scepticism; however, in the two years of running the programme, not one member of the team had lost their job. By following through on this promise, and skilling up her people with the right digital skills, mindset, and customer focus, she was able to galvanise trust in her team of around one hundred finance professionals. Now, the team not only actively uses the automation platform daily, but is voluntarily and proactively coming up with new ways to enhance workflows, which in turn removes complexity and manual tasks, and improves people's work/life balance.

Rachel went on to say that being armed with an inspired vision was important and made people feel they were part of something bigger than themselves. The company vision for this top tier bank was fondly described as a "202-year-old startup focused on being one of the greatest service businesses in the world," which clearly sets an energetic, digitally enabled, and agile focus. In addition, she had developed a clear strategy and, with these elements in place, was able to springboard from very strong foundations. By building trust and converting scepticism into curiosity, she was able to effectively engage her team and build confidence in the new technologies. Even if people did not have the skills initially, she was able to pique people's interest to proactively get more involved.

This chapter is about bringing the previous chapters all together and looks at the key elements that can help you create chain-reaction change management to help galvanise your digital evolution programme. This includes:

- What is chain reaction management?
- Why is it necessary?
- How do I achieve it?

WHAT IS CHAIN-REACTION CHANGE MANAGEMENT?

If you think of a business like a passenger liner, once it's moving at speed, you'll experience tremendous inertia if you want to change direction, even if only by a few degrees. It also takes the whole crew working together with a clear, unified goal to make everything work. In the same way, it's not easy to change direction for a business, but with the right foundations and application of your newly forming Digital EQ, you can successfully navigate any digital transformation or evolution.

Based on conversations I've had with many business leaders and pioneers, driving effective business transformations today requires demonstrating digitally savvy leadership and a well-developed Digital EQ. In these AI-fuelled times, there is likely to be uncertainty, anxiety, and confusion as people move away from the older, more manual ways of working towards newer, agile and more automated models, where developing new behaviours and skills will be essential to embrace the new world. So, it is important to have a leadership style that galvanises the right levels of trust in your strategy and ability to "steer the ship".

In the story above, we saw that the former IFAC President had established solid foundations to help her succeed. Having an inspired and purposeful vision, one which moves beyond shareholder returns, is sustainable and improves wider communities as well as having customer needs at its heart. In addition, coupled with a strategy that aligns people to achieve with a clear direction, it creates excitement and momentum. By instilling trust that she would support her people, she was able to bring them along the journey and shift gears from the old, more manual state to the new one. She was also able to give people a better quality of life and well-being as a result.

WHY DO YOU NEED CHAIN-REACTION CHANGE MANAGEMENT?

In the 2018 Deloitte Global Human Capital Trends survey and report of business and HR leaders, 72% indicated that AI, robots, and automation are important, but only 31% felt their organisations were prepared to address strategy to implement these technologies. Driving chain-reaction change management in companies that have less optimal legacy systems, siloed structures, skill gaps, and less nimble business models will be essential to giving transformation projects momentum and getting traction.

There is a tremendous amount of focus, investment, and commitment required to change behaviours and drive an inspired vision forward in any change management programme. Without trying to be the spectre of doom and gloom, depending on your programme's scale, without the catalyst of chain-reaction change management, your programme can be at risk of failing or falling short. I've personally seen it many times in a variety of businesses. With the right chain reaction, however, you can drive a programme like wildfire. Without it, you may get some results, but the fire smoulders and often fizzles out.

Ultimately, the end result is culture and brand erosions where your business could quickly disappear as staff and customers leave. It's a little like a rocket trying to leave the earth's atmosphere. If it doesn't have enough thrust behind it, inertia and gravity will drag the rocket back and it will stall, crash, and burn. When you're driving a department, business unit, or an organisation forward, you need to build positive momentum to fuel sustainable change.

To put on the Sydney Olympic Games required a small army of very engaged people focused on a common vision and goal – to build a better world through sport and deliver a world-class Olympic Experience. There wasn't sufficient budget for all the specialists required. Doctors, vets, medics, drivers, construction people, customer service people, and so on were required to run a two-week-long Olympic event. The Organising Committee needed an additional 42,000 volunteers to deliver the games. By building excitement and energy, over 46,000 volunteers came together and helped to deliver an incredible and memorable Olympic experience. The volunteers were a critical part of the Games. They were provided with good training, and when you met them, you could see they had a real sense of pride. Some were so engaged that they developed "the Olympic bug" and went on to follow Olympic Games in other countries to remain a part of the experience. Cherishing and celebrating the volunteers and making them feel valuable built a chain reaction of enthusiasm which spread like wildfire, creating an amazing experience for all who attended.

In our bank case study, the former president of IFAC demonstrated to her team that her people came first. She enabled them to build their skills and subsequent curiosity and trust to really embrace the new technologies. Without building chain-reaction change management, the programme could easily have stalled and failed to be effective.

> *I'm trying to build that skill in house. I didn't want to bring in outside support. I wanted the team to be encouraged through osmotic learning. They then tell others, and it grows from there.*
>
> —Rachel Grimes, Past President of IFAC

The risk in not building sufficient engagement and excitement to move your programmes along is that they may lose momentum and fizzle out, despite your best efforts. Using a surfing analogy, it's like riding a wave into shore. If the wave looks good, and has enough weight and force behind it, it will pick up enough speed and give you a great ride, carrying you back to the beach. However, if it's too small, it will fall short before you can get back home. Rallying teams of people requires that you can motivate, inspire, and support them to work together and change from one position to another, which may involve new technology, new approaches, and new ways of thinking outside their comfort zone. Building trust where people feel that automation may take their jobs, or trying to change a behaviour, like shifting from one way of learning to continuous learning, is no small thing and requires continuous focus and investment in time and effort. However, if you make the investment, the rewards are well worth the effort.

HOW DO YOU BUILD CHAIN-REACTION CHANGE MANAGEMENT FOR A DIGITAL EVOLUTION PROGRAMME?

There is no silver bullet to building the right level of enthusiasm for a change management programme, but, if you have a strong framework around your programme built on trust, clear focus, and rewarding people along the way, you should be able to create the right buy-in to shift your business from where it is now to where you want it to be. People generally don't like too much change all at once, so be sure to step your programme and set appropriate and achievable goals.

While there are many ways to build enthusiasm levels through business transformations or evolutions, the six core elements that pioneers and leaders use to drive successful chain-reaction change are highlighted in the asset below.

ASSET 10.1: CHAIN-REACTION CHANGE MANAGEMENT HEALTH CHECK METER

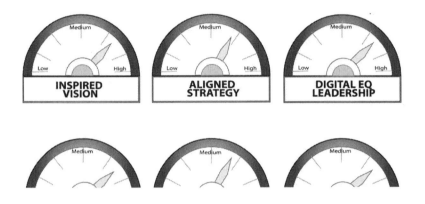

INSPIRED VISION: If your vision doesn't resonate or inspire, then it can be an uphill battle trying to digitally evolve or transform your business from the beginning. Having an inspired vision is important for people to feel they belong to something bigger than themselves; to inspire people to go the extra mile because they want to, rather than being asked to. If people aren't inspired, they're generally not on board, and when the going gets tough, there are less reasons to stay committed to the path.

Netflix, for example, has an inspired vision and mission. Their vision is "to continue being one of the leading firms of the internet entertainment era". It's simple, clear, easy to recall, with solid market leadership overtones. Their vision is further enhanced with an infinitely simple, yet powerful mission: "to entertain the world". The mission is equally simple, elegant, and inspiring. All in all, it provides clear direction as to what the vision of the business is, and its reason for being. As a result, it sets a clear direction that inspires.

In a shareholder letter, Jeff Bezos, former CEO of Amazon, drives inspiration as he talks about day one companies versus day two companies. He defines "day one" companies as those companies that are at the beginning of their potential. A "day two" company has a mindset that means stagnation followed by painful decline and death. Bezos wanted Amazon to retain its mindset as a "day one" company and endeavoured to create a culture that inspires people to that end.

> *Staying in day one requires you to experiment patiently, accept failures, plant seeds, protect saplings, and double down when you see customer delight. A customer-obsessed culture best creates the conditions where all of that can happen.*
>
> —Jeff Bezos, former CEO, Amazon

TIP: Develop an inspired vision and mission, or whatever guiding light works for your organisation, to help focus and steer the ship and establish clear business objectives. A quick way to test this is to look at your staff engagement surveys around vision and values or do your own toe-in-the-water research. Ask people in the business if they can tell you the vision. If they can, then that's a good start and hopefully it's a response to build an emotional connection on. If not and they just don't know, then the executives need to focus on finessing the vision so that it's easy to recall, emotionally driven, and inspirational.

ALIGNED STRATEGY: It's important in any change management programme that there is a clear strategy that is aligned across the business, that the strategy has clear ownership by the business leaders, and that it's aligned throughout the organisation. If the strategy is clear and transparent, people will better understand how their efforts contribute value back into the master plan. Tying it together and painting a clear and compelling story helps to solidify trust in the direction and the leadership – trust that the strategy is sound and sustainable, and trust that people's efforts will make a difference and help propel the business and their careers forward to greater heights. Without a clear, aligned strategy, people tend to lose enthusiasm and trust.

TIP: Demonstrate a strong, aligned strategy that is agile, clear, and built for the new digital age customer. Often, business divisions may not work collaboratively together because of their siloed structure. It's important that the divisions unite and drive integrated solutions. Prove ROI through pilot programmes, then look at the wider picture and how scaling could work. A good way to look at this is to have connectivity and a clear line of sight through the business from the top down and bottom up. Having integrated KPIs at the executive level that feed directly from the business strategy will help establish a framework to deliver a more aligned strategy.

DIGITAL EQ LEADERSHIP: You need a strong Digital EQ to manage through any digital transformation process, in which you can apply digital empathy and an understanding of the tech and new platforms. In our banking example, by putting her people first and following through to skill them up to new technologies, Rachel was able to deliver a successful programme, but stressed that if you cannot motivate by building momentum through curiosity and establishing trust, the teams will simply drop anchor. Another CFO I spoke with put it a different way, stating:

> *If you use a mallet and hit a nail hard enough and often enough, the nail will go into the wood eventually. But if you use smarter tools and the right approach to get engagement and buy-in, you unlock the full value of an organisation. Given the level of change in many digital transformation programmes, it needs to be end-to-end and involve people to achieve sustainable success.*
>
> —Raymond Jack, Executive Director, Commercial ACCA

A successful sustainable programme takes time to build and generally doesn't happen overnight, often because most people generally don't like change. It's human nature and takes time for people to trust any new way of doing something, particularly when they've been doing things a certain way over an extended period of time. If you recall from the earlier chapters, to master and build your Digital EQ, you need to build the five key pillars.

Once you have developed these pillars, you will be better equipped to cast a digital lens over your core business and be a more effective leader in this digital age.

> **TIP:** Digital leadership is not something that happens overnight; it takes time and commitment to build. One way to achieve this is to develop a continuously learning mindset for you and your team. Build on the skills you have and start to educate yourself across the myriad courses, information, white papers, blogs, and content that are now available digitally. To develop strong Digital EQ leadership, you need to have a sound grasp of the five key pillars we've outlined in this book.

SPARK CURIOSITY: Sparking people's curiosity is a great way to get people engaged and involved. When I spoke with the former President of IFAC, she shared this view:

> *The first thing is about people. Bringing people along the journey. So, my aim is to make people curious, then for them to embrace it, then tell somebody else. So, scale will come as people have ideas. They put their hand up for an idea. They see you haven't made anyone redundant, and trust develops. The scale comes when you have people who want to be involved.*
>
> —Rachel Grimes, Past President of IFAC

> **TIP:** Build curiosity to get people engaged and involved, which is the cornerstone to creating a groundswell and chain reaction. Encourage people to take ownership and drive the programme proactively. A good way to do this is to ask questions and get people in your teams to do the same. Identify team members who are more naturally curious and enlist them to help fuel the fires. If it is a brand transformation project, then identify brand advocates. If you build it right, the curiosity will build and gain momentum.

WELL-BEING IMPROVES PEOPLE'S LIVES: When people experience the tangible impact and value created as part of a digital transformation and see how it actually improves their quality of life, engagement starts to become genuine. The tangible impact can be as simple as leaving work on time rather than at

10 p.m. at month end or turning a laborious manual three-week process into a ten-minute automated customer experience. When people see the red tape start to disappear, inefficient processes fall away, customer solutions materialise that could never before be acted upon in a timely manner, or repetitive manual tasks be removed and picked up by bots, it improves people's lives and not only builds trust, but helps galvanise people to your vision.

> *As people move through this process, they realise the capacity they have to improve themselves. When people come into the office or log in remotely and they hit the button on their computer, there is so much data that it can take hours before they can actually use their screens. It's not efficient and it's not great for their work/life balance. So, having a robot free up that time, give them back those hours and get them to leave work on time, gives me the greatest satisfaction. What's happened is we have advocates to identify opportunities for robots and we have people saying now, 'my life has never been better.'*
>
> —Rachel Grimes, Past President of IFAC

So, if what you put into something is what you get out, put your people first and strive to create a better quality of life for your most valuable assets – your people.

TIP: It's important to show people the value of the digital change to answer the questions "what's in it for me?" and "what are the real benefits for me?" If it's a digital transformation project, then create a centre of excellence and have this team build excitement with the wider organisation through demonstrations and sharing how new technology, automation, or new platforms can really improve their daily experience at work as well as their work/life balance. Improving processes to be more efficient, removing red tape to make things easier, and replacing painful, time-consuming, labour-intensive tasks with automation to free people up to do more valuable programmes all go towards improving a person's mental health and well-being.

INSTIL TRUST: The first big question that needs to be addressed for employees is generally "will we be replaced by machines or algorithms?" To instil trust, take a "put your people first" approach and upskill, train, and/or redeploy them to areas more suited to their skills or learning styles. Clearly, the devil is in the detail, and defining what their new roles will look like in the new business models and how the teams will go about upskilling are all important aspects to consider. In our Multibillion-dollar Global Insurance Company case study in Chapter 3, the head of global funds ensured that he spent a great deal of time working with his team to help them understand what was in it for them. As a result, his team was able to see the value and that a great deal of repetitive, manual tasks would be removed from their lives and picked up by the fondly named Batman and Robin's bot overnight. By redesigning their position descriptions he was able to demonstrate value and instil trust.

From a business perspective, our CFO from AMP Capital built a fees and billing business case and proof of concept, which, when deployed, paid for itself quickly, delivering over six thousand manual hours back to the business and millions in revenue. This helped build trust that the automation process had value and did yield some great results.

From a customer perspective, with the need for trust more important than ever and data being processed out of sight, instilling trust is vital. The ability to build trust in a digital era, where we see increasing cyber-attacks in our big-data world, will have its challenges. If we consider the introduction of automated teller machines (ATMs) into banks a few decades ago, we saw how people responded to dealing with machines, albeit ATMs in the wall rather than AI-fuelled algorithms. In research conducted by the large banks at the time, when people were asked if they were happy to transact with a machine in the wall rather than a person, the response at the time was a resounding "NO!" followed by "How can we trust a machine?" and "I'd prefer to talk to a real person." People didn't trust machines and felt more comfortable speaking to a human. Now, fast-forward a few decades and we can see things have changed. Bank transactions are mainly via mobile phone through payment gateways, through banking apps, or on other electronic devices. As technology and cybersecurity improved, so too did consumer trust build over time. There is a need for the modern business to be digitally savvy and to deal with a more modern approach, so as digital transformations increase, instilling trust will be a vital part of success.

> **TIP:** Build trust through strong leadership. Follow through on promises made and demonstrate that the business has the capacity to deliver on the vision. Too often in change programmes, trust is unravelled quickly if the communications are overly scripted and not genuine or end up changing narrative. Build a transparent and accountable governance for AI-related matters and plan your progress to avoid "change saturation" and team burnout. Develop a heightened ethical framework that embraces the digital and a mature cybersecurity approach to help build safety and trust. Physically demonstrate that these changes will not only improve customer experiences but also improve your people's lives.

For the customer, this could be speeding up the purchase cycle or providing an intuitive user experience that takes some of the work away from the customer. For your staff, this could be going home on time at month end or freeing up their time by removing manual, robotic tasks for a much more seamless process without all the red tape. It's important that you "show them the money" and demonstrate tangible value. As with any project, take the time to understand how digital transformation impacts other projects and how to ensure you have an aligned and prioritised strategy.

EXERCISE 9 – BUILDING CHAIN-REACTION CHANGE MANAGEMENT

This short exercise below should help frame your thinking around areas you can focus on to get greater traction with your transformation or change management programme. Go to www.taketherobotoutofthehuman.com/exercises to download. If you apply these basic principles, it should help inform and shape your own programme.

SUMMARY: PART 3

CHAPTER 8: FLEX YOUR NEW DIGITAL MUSCLES TO REBUILD YOUR BUSINESS CORE

All businesses are different and at various stages of development. However, to review your core and drive a successful transformation or evolution, consider looking closely at the following six core pillars:

BUSINESS MODEL TRANSFORMATION: To meet the growing needs of consumers, new competitive pressures, and global pivots, business models need to be adaptable and flexible, so they can scale and be effective in meeting expectations in the new digital era. Look at your business model in light of your vision, digital strategy, Digital EQ, and customer-focused offerings.

TECHNICAL AND INFRASTRUCTURE READINESS: As businesses evolve from legacy-based platforms to something more agile and nimble, it's vital that technical and infrastructure readiness is in place. Review your technical capability and infrastructure in line with your vision and customer needs.

DATA ACCESS, AGILITY, AND CYBER PROTECTION: Having data that is accurate, accessible, and usable will become the foundation for the future. It's about rethinking your data strategy and thinking broadly. Consider your data strategy in line with customer needs. It's essential that effective and robust cybersecurity measures are put in place to protect your data, as well as the privacy of your customers to maintain trust.

FLUID STRATEGY AND MEASUREMENT: As business models change, so too should the strategy and measurement metrics to be fluid and flexible. Take a look at your existing strategy to identify where your business is going and what the strategy looks like to get there while staying relevant. Then, develop a flexible strategy and customer-centric measurements that drive business growth and customer satisfaction.

ETHICS AND REGULATORY COMPLIANCE: It's important to maintain trust in a new, digital world. Assess your ethics framework and compliance strategy to see if they are robust enough for all your stakeholders and customers.

SUSTAINABLE GROWTH: It's important to deliver the right revenue, community, and environmental value creation and growth. Build your Digital EQ to do this, as when your Digital EQ grows, so does your level of digital effectiveness and sophistication.

CHAPTER 9: HEIGHTENED ETHICS IN A DIGITAL WORLD

Having a clear and robust ethical framework as the business world becomes more digitally enabled is crucial. As cognitive machine-learning algorithms become more commonplace, and interpreting and analysing data is done through automated processes in "black boxes", there is a demand for a heightened ethical framework across businesses, from the board, the executives, and through to employees and partners to ensure trust. With a secure ethical framework, you can trust in the capture and use of information. You can trust that the storage and analysis of that data ensures that it is fair with no bias. You can trust that humans are in the loop and not shut out of the process. You can trust that the right level of expertise and security has been set up to ensure that the algorithms can't be compromised, and the data is safe and protected.

As the adoption of cognitive AI is relatively new in uses across businesses, more robust ethical frameworks will no doubt continue to develop and improve over time. However, there are good examples available now to help you develop the basis for a sound framework.

The following six topics outline the key area of focus:

HUMAN, SOCIAL, AND ENVIRONMENTAL WELL-BEING: Ensure in all instances that maintaining human, social, and environmental well-being is central to your ethical framework.

HUMANS AND AI: As robots and/or algorithms take up more of the repetitive manual tasks and higher cognitive, big-data type function, it's important that humans remain at the centre of the decision-making process. This way, AI enhances human intelligence rather than replacing it. Ensure you build humans into the loop as you develop your processes, platforms, and business models.

CONTINUOUS BIAS TESTING: Having bias creep into data, analysis, or AI processes is often inevitable, so it's important to build continuous bias testing into your processes and programmes to ensure fairness and mitigate bias.

ACCOUNTABILITY AND TRANSPARENCY: With AI automation comes the need for accountability for what the algorithm is doing, as well as heightened transparency to build trust with stakeholders, partners, customers, and employees. Build accountability and transparency into your governance and ensure it exists across the business from the board, the execs, senior management, and employees.

PRIVACY AND DATA INTEGRITY: As more businesses become data-driven, the need for privacy and integrity measures increases. Ensuring that you're acting in the best interests of individuals and society will be important to maintain trust with customers, partners, and shareholders.

TECHNICAL ROBUSTNESS AND SECURITY: Develop the right technical knowledge and understanding to explain the decision-making process for learning algorithms. Ensure that the right cybersecurity measures are in place to protect the platforms.

CHAPTER 10: CHAIN-REACTION CHANGE MANAGEMENT

To achieve results and the best chance for success, it's important to bring it all together now that you're on the road to building Digital EQ. Building chain-reaction change management and getting others on board as advocates propels and drives momentum and scale.

SET STRONG FOUNDATIONS – INSPIRED VISION, INTEGRATED STRATEGY, AND CLEAR OBJECTIVES: If your foundations are solid, it sets the programme up for success. Take the time to ensure you can inspire people, demonstrate an integrated approach, and map out clear objectives for people to get behind.

SET REALISTIC LEVELS OF AMBITION – AVOID CHANGE OVERLOAD: Some organisations struggle to successfully launch their business into the stratosphere. Instead, they overcommit and inevitably fall short. As people generally don't like wholesale change, focusing on specific core programmes can be a more palatable option.

LEAD BY EXAMPLE – LEARN THE PLATFORMS AND AI TECHNOLOGIES: When you're leading a digital transformation, it's important to know the fundamentals of the technology. It doesn't mean you need to become a coder, but it's important to understand the platforms, do the research, and educate yourself on the principles, terminology, and capabilities. Build your Digital EQ to effectively lead.

PUT YOUR PEOPLE FIRST – FIX SKILL GAPS AND PREPARE THEM FOR THE JOURNEY: People will be working with smart machines, algorithms, new platforms, and AI-driven technologies. This means that employees, senior management, and boards will need to develop continuous new skills, behaviours, and even mindsets. Put your people first – invest in their futures and they will invest in yours.

DEVELOP ROBUST AI, HEIGHTENED ETHICS, AND CYBERSECURITY GOVERNANCE WITH END-TO-END TRANSPARENCY: In the new big-data, AI-fuelled world where data will be the major currency to drive customer insights, product modification, and value creation, having a strong governance structure around ethics, AI, and cybersecurity will be really important.

FLEX YOUR DIGITAL LEADERSHIP MUSCLES – EXERCISE EMPATHY AROUND NEW TECHNOLOGY AND RAPID CHANGE: With new technology, new behaviours, and rapid change will come confusion and challenges. Ensuring you have the right level of digital empathy will be important to manage digital and human workforces working hand-in-hand with new technology.

NEED MORE HELP FOR YOU AND YOUR BUSINESS?

My ambition for writing this book was to provide five simple pillars that, when applied, will help you and your teams become more uniquely human and more relevant as we move into the next digital decade. This will help you to develop stronger soft skills and become more successful as automation, robots and AI ultimately remove the repetitive and mundane tasks in our working lives. Ultimately, it will help you build the right behaviours and even adopt a modern entrepreneurial spirit that will be vital to manage through the pivots, twists and turns in this new era.

If you would like help building your Digital EQ, or building effective digital evolution programmes and strategies, you can visit our website at www.taketherobotoutofthehuman.com/exercises for worksheets, tips and tools, or book a consultation for a tailor-made programme. You can also follow us on Instagram, Twitter and LinkedIn.

If you are after a speaker, I would be delighted to attend your event or virtual event to deliver a compelling perspective on being human and value creation in this new digital age.

I do hope you have found this book useful to develop the right mindsets, behaviours, relationships, skills and focus, ultimately establishing the foundations that allow you to weather digital storms and thrive as a result.

ABOUT THE AUTHOR

With a background founded in Australian law, global brand development, and credentials from Harvard Business School, Julian's focus over the next decade is helping businesses with digital and NetZero value creation transformations.

Julian has decades of experience as a senior executive across a range of business sectors, including aerospace, banking and finance, professional accounting, telecommunications, insurance, and government. Julian helps businesses solve complex problems by applying a cross section of disciplines and thinking styles gained through broad ecosystems thinking.

For more than a decade, Julian has been speaking and hosting industry business events with government, accounting firms, universities, Deloitte, KPMG, the Association of Chartered Certified Accountants and with many other industries. If you would like to discuss speaking opportunities, you can reach him through the website or via LinkedIn.

SOURCES

CHAPTER 1: A CONVERGENCE – NOWHERE TO HIDE

Daugherty, P., Carrel-Billiard, M., and Blitz, M. (2020). We, the post-digital people. Can your enterprise survive the 'tech-clash'? Technology Vision, Accenture. Available at: https://www.accenture.com/us-en/insights/technology/technology-trends-2020

DX Technology. (2017). Digital Transformation is Racing Ahead, and No Industry is Immune. *Harvard Business Review*. Available at: https://hbr.org/sponsored/2017/07/digital-transformation-is-racing-ahead-and-no-industry-is-immune-2

Frey, C, Osborne, M. (2013). The Future of Employment: How susceptible are jobs to computerisation? University of Oxford. Available at: https://www.oxfordmartin.ox.ac.uk/downloads/academic/The_Future_of_Employment.pdf

Gurumurthy, R., and Schatsky, D. (2019). Pivoting to digital maturity. Seven capabilities central to digital transformation. Deloitte Insights. US. Available at: https://www2.deloitte.com/us/en/insights/focus/digital-maturity/digital-maturity-pivot-model.html

Halls, A. (2019). The meteor is coming – The role of the private equity backed CFO, Deloitte UK. Available at: https://www2.deloitte.com/content/dam/Deloitte/uk/Documents/private-markets/deloitte-uk-role-of-the-pe-backed-cfo-web.pdf

Harvard Business Review (2017). Digital Transformation Is Racing Ahead and No Industry Is Immune. Available at: https://hbr.org/sponsored/2017/07/digital-transformation-is-racing-ahead-and-no-industry-is-immune-2

LaBerge, L., O'Toole, C., Schneider J., and Smaje K. (2020). How COVID-19 has pushed companies over the technology tipping point – and transformed business forever. Available at: https://www.mckinsey.com/business-functions/strategy-and-corporate-finance/our-insights/how-covid-19-has-pushed-companies-over-the-technology-tipping-point-and-transformed-business-forever#

Lyon, J. (2020). Future ready: Accountancy careers in the 2020s. ACCA Insights, UK. Available at: https://www.accaglobal.com/in/en/professional-insights/pro-accountants-the-future/future_ready_2020s.html

Lyon, J. (2018). Embracing robotic automation during the evolution of finance. ACCA Insights, UK. Available at: https://www.accaglobal.com/lk/en/professional-insights/technology/embracing-robotic-automation-during-the-evolution-of-finance.html

Prinsloo, A. (2020). PREPARING FUTURE READY PROFESSIONALS. CA ANZ's Rapid Move to Online Exams and Beyond– A Case Study of Six Weeks from Start to Delivery. International Federation of Accountants. Available at: https://www.ifac.org/knowledge-gateway/preparing-future-ready-professionals/discussion/ca-anz-s-rapid-move-online-exams-and-beyond-case-study-six-weeks-start-delivery

Van Eerd, R. (2020). Jobs will be very different in 10 years. Here's how to prepare: Paris Hub. World Economic Forum. Available at: https://www.weforum.org/agenda/2020/01/future-of-work/

CHAPTER 2: USING DIGITAL EQ TO NAVIGATE CHANGE

Bughin, J., Hazan, E., Lund, S., Dahlström, P., Wiesinger, A., and Subramaniam, A.

(2018). Skills Shift: Automation and the future of the workforce. McKinsey Global Institute. Available at: https://www.mckinsey.com/featured-insights/future-of-work/skill-shift-automation-and-the-future-of-the-workforce

Dutta, D., Gillard, A., and Kaczmarskyj, G. (2016). Get ready for robots. Why planning makes the difference between success and disappointment. EY Global. UK. Available at: https://assets.ey.com/content/dam/ey-sites/ey-com/en_gl/topics/emeia-financial-services/ey-get-ready-for-robots.pdf

Gurumurthy, R., and Schatsky, D. (2019). Pivoting to digital maturity. Seven capabilities central to digital transformation. Deloitte Insights. US. Available at: https://www2.deloitte.com/us/en/insights/focus/digital-maturity/digital-maturity-pivot-model.html

CHAPTER 3: SKILLS AND CONTINUOUS LEARNING

Baig, A., Hall, B., Jenkins, P., Lamarre, E., and McCarthy, B. (2020). The COVID-19 recovery will be digital: A plan for the first 90 days. McKinsey Article.

Brauer, C., Barth, J., Golan, M., Gaspar, M., Ahern, C., Samaranik A., Moretti, L., King, S., and Leizaola, R. (2017). Artificial Intelligence & the Freedom to be Human. FuturaCorp. A research collaboration between IPsoft and researchers at Goldsmiths, University of London and independent research firm Smoothmedia. Available at: https://www.ipsoft.com/wp-content/uploads/2017/01/FuturaCorp.pdf?submissionGuid=9d67861b-0cd9-4ef4-88ad-b7246a65ae53

Bryson, J. (2020). The Future of Work – A vision for IFAC members. Available at: https://www.ifac.org/knowledge-gateway/preparing-future-ready-professionals/discussion/future-work-vision-ifac-members

Bughin, J., Hazan, E., Lund, S., Dahlström, P., Wiesinger, A., and Subramaniam, A. (2018). Skills shift: Automation and the future of work. Discussion paper. McKinsey Global Institute. Available at: https://www.mckinsey.com/featured-insights/future-of-work/skill-shift-automation-and-the-future-of-the-workforce

Einstein, A. (1955). "The important thing is not to stop questioning. Curiosity has its own reason for existence. One cannot help but be in awe when he contemplates the mysteries of eternity, of life, of the marvellous structure of reality. It is enough if one tries merely to comprehend a little of this mystery each day. Never lose a holy curiosity." [quoted in, "Death of a Genius–Old Man's Advice to Youth: 'Never Lose a Holy Curiosity," *Life Magazine,* 38, no. 18, (May 2, 1955): p. 64].

Lyon, J. (2016). Professional Accountants – the Future: Drivers of Change and Skills. ACCA UK. Available at: https://www.accaglobal.com/gb/en/technical-activities/technical-resources-search/2016/june/professional-accountants-the-future-report.html

Lyon, J. (2016). Market Change is Faster than Ever – Is Your Finance Function in the Race? ACCA/PwC. Available at: https://www.accaglobal.com/gb/en/professional-insights/technology/market-change-is-faster-than-ever.html

PWC Network. (2020). Digital Fitness for the World App – PWC. Available at: https://www.pwc.com/us/en/products/digital-fitness.html

Manyika, J. (2017). Technology, jobs, and the future of work. Executive Briefing.

McKinsey Global Institute. Available at: https://www.
mckinsey.com/featured-insights/employment-and-growth/
technology-jobs-and-the-future-of-work

Moritz, R., Pénicaud, P., Hummelgaard, P., Morgan, J., Hagemann Snabe, J., Oreshkin, M., and Zahidi, S. (2020). Social Mobility. Reskilling the Next Billion. World Economic Forum. Available at: https://www.weforum.org/events/world-economic-forum-annual-meeting-2020/sessions/social-mobility-a-reskilling-revolution-for-the-next-billion

McKinsey Insights. (2020). Soft skills for Hard Work. McKinsey Quarterly. Available at: https://www.mckinsey.com/featured-insights/future-of-work/five-fifty-soft-skills-for-a-hard-world

Vaidyanathan, N. (2019). Machine Learning – More science than fiction. ACCA UK. Available at:
https://www.accaglobal.com/gb/en/professional-insights/technology/machine-learning.html

Webb, C. (2018). Learning for the Future. ACCA UK.
https://www.accaglobal.com/gb/en/professional-insights/pro-accountants-the-future/learning-for-the-future.html

Zahidi, S. (2020). We need a global reskilling revolution- here's why. World Economic Forum. Davos. Available at: https://www.weforum.org/agenda/2020/01/reskilling-revolution-jobs-future-skills/

CHAPTER 4: HUMAN (CUSTOMER) FOCUS

Baldoni, J. (2011). Lead with Purpose – Giving Your Organization a Reason to Believe in Itself. Amazon & Paperback Edition: New York.

Bersin, J. (2016). The New Organization: Different by Design. Available at: https://joshbersin.com/2016/03/the-new-organization-different-by-design/

Bognses, B. (2016). Implementing Beyond Budgeting: Unlocking the Performance Potential. 2nd edition. John Wiley & Sons: London.

Breuer, R., Fanderl, H., Freundt, T., Maechler, N, Moritz, S., and van der Marel, F. (2019). What matters in customer-experience transformations. McKinsey & Company Article. Available at: https://www. mckinsey.com/business-functions/marketing-and-sales/our-insights/ what-matters-in-customer-experience-cx-transformations

Sandlin, D. (2015). Backwards Bicycle Brain – Smarter every day 133. YouTube. Available here: https://www.youtube.com/watch?v=MFzDaBzBlL0

Easterbrook, S. President & CEO, McDonalds Corporation. (2019). McDonald's to Acquire Dynamic Yield, Will Use Decision Technology to Increase Personalization and Improve Customer Experience. Available at: https:// corporate.mcdonalds.com/corpmcd/en-us/our-stories/article/ourstories. dynamic_yield.html

Edin, P., Serenbetz, T. (2019). Succeeding as a CFO in a Digital world. Lessons Learned from the CFOs of 100 leading Technology and Communications companies. Available at: https://advisory.kpmg.us/content/dam/advisory/en/ pdfs/succeeding-as-cfo-in-a-digital-world.pdf

Greco, M. Group Chief Executive Officer. (2019). Media release Zurich 14/11/2019 Available at: https://www.zurich.com/es-es/media/news-releases/2019/2019-1114-01

Guszcza, J., Lee, M., Ammanath, B., and Kuder, D. (2020). Human values in the loop: Design principles for ethical AI. Available at: https://www2.deloitte. com/uk/en/insights/focus/cognitive-technologies/design-principles-ethical-artificial-intelligence.html

Harris, S.D. (2009/2016). 2009 Q&A: Marc Benioff, CEO of Salesforce. com, Mercury News, 23 October (revised 16 August 2016). Available at: https://www.mercurynews. com/2009/10/23/2009-qa-marc-benioff-ceo-of-salesforce-com/

Kaji, J., Hurley, B., Gangopadhyay, N., Bhat, R., and Khan, A. (2019). Leading the social enterprise: Reinvent with a human focus (2019), Deloitte Global Human Capital Trends. Available at: https://www2.deloitte.com/content/dam/ insights/us/articles/5136_HC-Trends-2019/DI_HC-Trends-2019.pdf

Ovanessoff, A., Sage-Gavin, E., and Morvan, L. (2018). It's learning. Just not as we know it. Accenture article. Available at: https://www.accenture.com/us-en/ insights/future-workforce/transforming-learning

Taylor, B. (2018). To See the Future of Competition, Look at Netflix. *Harvard Business Review.* Available at: https://hbr.org/2018/07/ to-see-the-future-of-competition-look-at-netflix

Viki, T. (2018). The Three Human Barriers to Digital Transformation. Available at: https://www.forbes.com/sites/tendayiviki/2018/09/23/ the-three-human-barriers-to-digital-transformation/?sh=39851bab164b

CHAPTER 5: AMPLIFIED VALUE CREATION MINDSET

Anthony, S., Trotter, A., Schwartz, E. I. (2019). The Top 20 Business Transformations of the Last Decade. *Harvard Business Review.* Available at: https://hbr.org/2019/09/ the-top-20-business-transformations-of-the-last-decade

Benitez, L. (2018). Banco Popular bank case study. Available at: https://www. ibm.com/case-studies/banco-popular

Chaudhary, S. (2020). 'Emirati Queen Bee', for UAE's food security is here. World Bee initiative. Available at: https://gulfnews.com/uae/

emirati-queen-bee-for-uaes-food-security-is-here-1.69003342 Also visit http://worldbeeproject.org/

Charness, J. (2019). How Oracle and the World Bee Project are using AI to Save Bees. Oracle AI. Available at: https://blogs.oracle.com/datascience/how-oracle-and-the-world-bee-project-are-using-ai-to-save-bees-v2,

Chandra, S. (2019). University of Melbourne saves 10,000 hours annually with Automation Anywhere. Available at: https://www.automationanywhere.com/uk/case-study-univ-melbourne

Food and Agriculture Organisation of the United Nations article. (2019). Declining bee populations pose threat to global food security and nutrition. Food and Agriculture Organisation of the United Nations. Available at: http://www.fao.org/news/story/en/item/1194910/icode/, http://sos-bees.org/, https://blog-idcuk.com/saving-the-bees-with-big-data-analytics-and-ai/

Kedziora, D., and Kiviranta, H. (2018). Digital Business Value Creation with Robotic Process Automation (RPA) in Northern and Central Europe Article. ResearchGate article. Available at: https://www.researchgate.net/publication/328777883_Digital_Business_Value_Creation_with_Robotic_Process_Automation_RPA_in_Northern_and_Central_Europe

Jeffress, A. (2019). Australia Post optimises accounting workflows with RPA Bots. Automation Anywhere. Australia Post case study. Available at: https://www.automationanywhere.com/uk/casestudy-australia

Jobs, S. iPhone launch (2007). Steve Jobs iPhone presentation. YouTube. Available at: https://www.youtube.com/watch?v=vN4U5FqrOdQ

Ocado case study (2021). Corporate Social Responsibility (CSR) HUB and Environment, Social & Government ESG) metrics. Ocado Group. Available at: https://www.csrhub.com/CSR_and_sustainability_information/Ocado-Group-PLC

Ocado group. (2020). Strong performance in challenging times Interim results for the 26 weeks ended 31 May 2020. OCADO GROUP PLC. Available at: https://www.ocadogroup.com/sites/ocado-corp-v2/files/interim-financial-statements-1h-20-final-july.pdf

Steiner, T. (2018). Ocado Group CEO Tim Steiner on the key factors behind our success. Available at: https://www.youtube.com/watch?v=5ZB7KeLLmGo

Ocado website. (2021). Corporate Social Responsibility report. Available at: http://results12.ocadogroup.com/performance/corporate-social-responsibility-report.html

QuickBooks Canada Team. (2018). What is Blue Sky thinking? Available at: https://quickbooks.intuit.com/ca/resources/self-employed/blue-sky-thinking/

Kotzen, J., Rice, G., Gjerstad, K., Farag, H., Foldsey, J., Hansell, G., Kaku, I. (2021). Value Creation Strategy and Shareholder Activism Defense. BCG Corporate Finance and Strategy. Available at: https://www.bcg.com/capabilities/corporate-development-finance/value-creation-strategy.aspx

Walmart 2018 Global Responsibility Report Summary, Report by visiting corporate.walmart.com/2018GRR. Available at: https://corporate.walmart.com/media-library/document/2018-grr-summary/_proxyDocument?id=00000162-e4a5-db25-a97f-f7fd785a0001

World Bee Project Video. (2018). World Bee Project – How can technology solve the bee population decline? Report by the Intergovernmental Science-Policy Platform on Biodiversity and Ecosystem Services (IPBES). Available at: https://www.youtube.com/watch?v=L4CFpXhdE1Y

CHAPTER 6: PARTNERSHIPS AND ECOSYSTEMS

Barker, A. (2019). Lego's journey through digital innovation and beyond. IT Brief. Available at: https://itbrief.co.nz/story/lego-s-journey-through-digital-innovation-and-beyond

Bentonville A. (2017). Walmart Offers New Financial Wellness Services for Associates Nationwide. Available at: https://corporate.walmart.com/newsroom/2017/12/13/walmart-offers-new-financial-wellness-services-for-associates-nationwide

Farlinger, K., Global CEO at BDO, (2019). BDO's global revenues grow 10% to US$ 9.6bn. BDO United Kingdom: Available at: https://www.bdo.co.uk/en-gb/news/2019/bdos-global-financial-results

Hemmerle, A. (2019). Fast, efficient, reliable: Artificial intelligence in BMW Group Production. Press release. Available at: https://www.press.bmwgroup.com/global/article/detail/T0298650EN/fast-efficient-reliable:-artificial-intelligence-in-bmw-group-production?language=en

Jordan, J., Sorell, M. (2019). Why You Should Create a "Shadow Board" of Younger Employees. *Harvard Business Review.* Available at: https://hbr.org/2019/06/why-you-should-create-a-shadow-board-of-younger-employees

Justice, C. (2020). Intelligent automation KPMG alliance partners . Available at: https://advisory.kpmg.us/articles/2018/intelligent-automation-kpmg-alliance-partners.html

Lang, N., von Szczepanski, K., Wurzer, C. (2019). The Emerging Art of Ecosystem Management, Boston Consulting Group. Available at: https://www.bcg.com/en-gb/publications/2019/emerging-art-ecosystem-management

Lyman, M., Ref, R., Wright, O. (2018). Corner Stone of Future Growth ECOSYSTEMS. Accenture. Available at: https://www.accenture.com/_acnmedia/pdf-77/accenture-strategy-ecosystems-exec-summary-may2018-pov.pdf

Mitchell, M. (2018). Netflix Looks to Partnerships for Growth. No Plans for Live Sport. Available at: https://variety.com/2018/tv/news/netflix-looks-partnerships-growth-no-plans-live-sport-1202942082/

Portincaso, M., del la Tour, A., and Soussan, P. (2019). The Dawn of the Deep Tech Ecosystem. BCG, March 2019. Available at: https://www.bcg.com/capabilities/digital-technology-data/emerging-technologies/deep-tech

Prins, N. (2015). The Spotify – Starbucks Partnership Is Digital Co-Branding Genius. *Forbes.* Available at: https://www.forbes.com/sites/nomiprins/2015/05/19/the-spotify-starbucks-partnership-is-digital-co-branding-genius/#2cfe509f4a7a

Ringel, M., Kennedy, D., Manly, J., Baeza, R., and Spira, M. (2019). The Most Innovative Companies, The Rise of AI, Platforms, and Ecosystems. BCG. Available at: https://www.bcg.com/en-us/publications/collections/most-innovative-companies-2019-artificial-intelligence-platforms-ecosystems

Ringel, M., Baeza, R., and Manly, J. (2019). How Collaborative Platforms and Ecosystems Are Changing Innovation The Most Innovative Companies 2019. Available at: https://www.bcg.com/en-us/publications/2019/most-innovative-companies-collaborative-platforms-ecosystems-changing-nnovation

Schroeck, M., Kwan, A., Gill, J., and Sharma, D. (2020). Evolving partner roles in Industry 4.0. Available at: https://www2.deloitte.com/us/en/insights/focus/industry-4-0/partner-ecosystem-industry-4-0.html

Susskind, R., and Susskind, D. (2015). The Future of the Professions: How technology will transform the work of the human experts (Oxford, 2015). p.117–18 & 267–68.

Wu, C., and Han, J. (2019). 12 Innovations that Will Change Health Care and Medicine in the 2020s. Available at: https://time.com/5710295/top-health-innovations/

CHAPTER 7: ENTREPRENEURIAL (MODERN) SPIRIT

Ford, H. (1923). "Be ready to revise any system, scrap any method, abandon any theory, if the success of the job requires it." Subject: Pride Source: Ford News, p. 2. Date: 1/15/1923.

Harris, S.D. (2009/2016). 2009 Q&A: Marc Benioff, CEO of Salesforce.com, *Mercury News,* 23 October (revised 16 August 2016). Available at: https://www.mercurynews.com/2009/10/23/2009-qa-marc-benioff-ceo-of-salesforce- com/

Kerr, S., Kerr, W., and Xu, T. (2017). Personality Traits of Entrepreneurs: A Review of Recent Literature, Harvard Business School, Working paper 18-047. Harvard Business School. Available at: https://www.hbs.edu/ris/Publication%20Files/18-047_b0074a64-5428-479b-8c83-16f2a0e97eb6.pdf

Kubler-Ross, E. (1969). On Death and Dying (Routledge: New York). Pink, D. (2009) Drive: The Surprising Truth About What Motivates Us (Riverhead Books: New York).

Revzin, S., Revzin, V. (2018). How to Encourage Entrepreneurial Thinking on Your Team, Sergei Revzin, Vadim Revzin December 21, 2018. Harvard Business Review. Available at: https://hbr.org/2018/12/how-to-encourage-entrepreneurial-thinking-on-your-team

Schawbel, D. (2013). The Re-Definition of Entrepreneurship and Rise of Freedom-Seeking Freelancers. *Forbes.* Available at: https://www.forbes.com/sites/danschawbel/2013/05/14/the-re-definition-of-entrepreneurship-and-rise-of-freedom-seeking-freelancers/?sh=10996a776a99

Schumpeter, J. A. (1912). The Theory of Economic Development, tenth printing 2004, Transaction Publishers, New Brunswick, New Jersey.

CHAPTER 8: FLEX YOUR NEW DIGITAL MUSCLES TO REBUILD YOUR BUSINESS CORE

Australia Post Annual Report (2019). Available at: https://auspost.com.au/content/dam/auspost_corp/media/documents/ publications/2019-australia-post-annual-report.pdf

Australia Post case study. (2017). Enabling Australia Post's digital Future with Scaled Agile Framework. Australia. Available at: https://www.scaledagileframework.com/wp-content/uploads/ delightful-downloads/2017/11/Australia-Post-SAFe-Case-Study-v1.0.pdf

Bastone, N. (2019). Elon Musk Says Tesla Will Roll Out 1 Million Robo-Taxis by Next Year. Here's How He Plans on Doing It. Inc. article. Available at: https://www.inc.com/business-insider/tesla-is-taking-direct-aim-at-uber-and-lyft-with-plans-to-roll-out-one-million-robo-taxis-by-next-year.html

Beuhler, K., Anant, V., Bailey, T., Kaplan, J., Nayfeh, M., Richter, W. (2020). Cybersecurity in a Digital Era. Digital McKinsey and Global Risk Practice. Available at: https://www.mckinsey.com/~/media/McKinsey/ Business%20Functions/Risk/Our%20Insights/Cybersecurity%20in%20a%20 digital%20era/Cybersecurity%20in%20a%20Digital%20Era.pdf

Brosseau, D., Ebrahim, S., Handscomb, C., and Thaker, S. (2019). Journey to an agile organisation. McKinsey & Company Article. Available at: https:// www.mckinsey.com/business-functions/organization/our-insights/ the-journey-to-an-agile-organization#

Close, K., Grebe, M., Schuuring, M., Rehberg, B., and Leybold, M. (2020). Anatomy of the bionic company BCG the successful company will blend human and technological capabilities. BCG. Available at: https://www.bcg.com/ featured-insights/winning-the-20s/anatomy-of-the-bionic-company.aspx

Close, K., Grebe, M., Schuuring, M., Rehberg, B., and Leybold, M. (2020). – Is your technology Ready for a new digital reality? BCG Article. Available at: https://www.bcg.com/publications/2020/is-technology-ready-new-digital-reality-post-covid19.aspx?utm_medium=Email&utm_source=esp&utm_campaign=covid&utm_description=ealert&utm_topic=none&utm_geo=global&utm_content=202006&utm_usertoken=CRM_c86a2139a96f285d0d9ddbd3edabf60d47244238&redir=true

Crozier, R. (2019). Australia Post tackles 'observability' after digital transformation. IT News. https://www.itnews.com.au/news/australia-post-tackles-observability-after-digital-transformatin-533816

Erickson, R., Moulton, D., Cleary, B. (2020). Are you overlooking your greatest talent? Deloitte Review. Available at: https://www2.deloitte.com/content/dam/insights/us/collections/issue-23/DI-Deloitte-Review-23.pdf.

Gurumurthy, R., and Schatsky , D. (2019). Pivoting to digital maturity. Seven capabilities central to digital transformation. Deloitte insights. Available at: https://www2.deloitte.com/us/en/insights/focus/digital-maturity/digital-maturity-pivot-model.html

Osipovich, A. (2020). Tesla Stock Rides Seven-Session Winning Streak, Rising 56%. *The Wall Street Journal.* Available at: https://www.wsj.com/articles/tesla-stock-rides-seven-session-winning-streak-rising-more-than-60-11586883627

Simon, M. (2019). Inside the Amazon Warehouse Where Humans and Machines Become One. *Wired.* Available at: https://www.wired.com/story/amazon-warehouse-robots/

Subramanian, A. (2020). Philips Case Study. With thanks to Philips, edgeverve and infosystems for their webinar, 2020. Available at: https://www.youtube.com/watch?v=1ys-bdljWpI

Timm, C. (2019). Australia Post delivers online and in-person for customers. Google Cloud. Article. Available at: https://cloud.google.com/blog/topics/customers/australia-post-delivers-online-and-in-person-for-customers

Wallington, I. (2018). Innovate or perish: An interview with Australia Post Leaders. Futuregov. Rick Wingfield (Partner, Australia Post Accelerate) and Gary Starr (GM Enterprise & Government Solutions, Trusted eCommerce Services). Available at: https://blog.wearefuturegov.com/innovate-or-perish-an-interview-with-australia-post-service-leaders-d4b080eb98dc

WHICH-50 Insight. (2019). Australia Post TO Future Proof Services with Telco Transformation. Available at: https://which-50.com/australia-post-to-future-proof-services-with-telco-transformation/

CHAPTER 9: HEIGHTENED ETHICS IN A DIGITAL WORLD

Anderson, M. (2017). After 75 years, Isaac Asimov's Three Laws of Robotics need updating. The Conversation Trust. Available at: https://theconversation.com/after-75-years-isaac-asimovs-three-laws-of-robotics-need-updating-74501

Bossmann, J. (2016). Top 9 ethical issues in artificial intelligence. World Economic Forum. Alumni, Global Shapers Community, Fathom Computing. Available at: https://www.weforum.org/agenda/2016/10/top-10-ethical-issues-in-artificial-intelligence

Bryson, J. (2020). On Regulating the Software behind Artificial Intelligence. Big Tech. Available at: https://www.cigionline.org/big-tech/joanna-j-bryson-regulating-software-behind-artificial-intelligence/

Bradley, A. (2020). 4 stages of Ethical AI: Algorithm bias is not the problem, it's part of the solution. Gartner blog post. Available at: https://blogs.gartner.com/anthony_bradley/2020/01/15/4-stages-ethical-ai-algorithmic-bias-not-problem-part-solution/

Buolamwini, J., and Gebru, T., (2018). Gender Shades: Intersectional Accuracy Disparities in Commercial Gender Classification. MIT media Lab. Proceedings of the 1st Conference on Fairness, Accountability and Transparency, PMLR 81:77-91, 2018. Available at:

https://www.media.mit.edu/publications/gender-shades-intersectional-accuracy-disparities-in-commercial-gender-classification/

Davenport, T., and Katyal, V. (2018). Every Leader's guide to the Ethics of AI. MIT Sloan Management Review. Available at: https://sloanreview.mit.edu/article/every-leaders-guide-to-the-ethics-of-ai/?gclid=CjwKCAjwrcH3BRApEiwAxjdPTR-mVtOhQA42j4UQd_CoEdZsHBFSnk7xfhTn0X8nuQkOk1QtoxVUURoCHIoQAvD_BwE#article-authors

Eckersley, P. (2018). How good Are Google's new AI ethics principles? Electronic Frontier Foundation. Available at: https://www.eff.org/deeplinks/2018/06/how-good-are-googles-new-ai-ethics-principles

Elish, M. (2020). Who is responsible when autonomous systems fail? Centre for International Governance Innovation. Available at: https://www.cigionline.org/articles/who-responsible-when-autonomous-systems-fail/

Floridi, L. (2013). The Ethics of Information. Luciano Floridi Professor of Philosophy and Ethics of Information, Director of the Digital Ethics Lab, Oxford Internet Institute, University of Oxford. Available at: https://global.oup.com/academic/product/the-ethics-of-information-9780199641321?cc=gb&lang=en&

Friedrich, B., and Friedrich, L. (2019). The place for bias in the future of accounting. Banishing machine bias requires human self-awareness. Brian Friedrich, board member at the International Ethics Standard Board for Accountants (IESBA). *Canadian Accountant.* Available at:

http://www.canadian-accountant.com/content/business/
the-place-for-bias-in-the-future-of-accounting

Friedrich, B., and Friedrich, L. (2019). Guardians of trust in the Age
of AI – Our ethical foundations will secure our place in the future.
Available at: http://www.canadian-accountant.com/content/business/
accountants-guardians-of-trust-in-the-age-of-ai

Guszcza, J., Lee, M., Ammanath, B., and Kuder, D. (2020). Human values in
the loop: Design principles for ethical AI. Available at: https://www2.deloitte.
com/uk/en/insights/focus/cognitive-technologies/design-principles-ethical-
artificial-intelligence.html

Hussey, L., Taylor, B., and Murdoch, H. (2018). AI in the UK: Ready Willing
& Able. House of Lords Select Committee on Artificial Intelligence Report
Session 2017-19. House of Lords UK. Available at: https://publications.
parliament.uk/pa/ld201719/ldselect/ldai/100/100.pdf

Krishna, D., Albinson, N., and Chi, Y. (2017). Managing algorithmic risks.
Safeguarding the use of complex algorithms and machine learning. Deloitte.
Available at: https://www2.deloitte.com/us/en/pages/risk/articles/
algorithmic-machine-learning-risk-management.html

Mulvaney, T., Driscoll, G., Friedrich, B., Fukukawa, H., and Madden, M.
IESBA working group (2019). IESBA Technology Initiative, Phase 1 Final
Report December 2019. Available at: https://www.ifac.org/system/files/
publications/files/IESBA-Technology-Initiative-Phase-1-Final-Report_0.pdf

Pichai, S. (2018). AI at Google: our principles. Google Article. Available
at: https://blog.google/topics/ai/ai-principles/.

Smith, R. (2018). 5 Core principles to keep AI ethical. World Economic
Forum. Available at: https://www.weforum.org/agenda/2018/04/
keep-calm-and-make-ai-ethical/

Syal, D. (2019). It's time to stop talking about ethics in AI and start doing it. World Economic Forum report. Available at: https://www.weforum.org/agenda/2019/01/it-s-time-to-stop-talking-about-ethics-in-ai-and-start-doing-it/. World Economic Forum. BCG Digital Ventures

Vaccarono, F. (2019). A new tool to help Italian companies grow with AI. Available at: https://www.blog.google/outreach-initiatives/grow-with-google/machine-learning-checkup-italy/

CHAPTER 10: CHAIN-REACTION CHANGE MANAGEMENT

Davenport, T., Locks J., and Schatsky D. (2017). Deloitte state of cognitive technologies survey – Get insights from early adopters of cognitive and AI. Available at: https://www2.deloitte.com/us/en/pages/deloitte-analytics/articles/cognitive-technology-adoption-survey.html

Kane, G., Palmer, D., Phillips, A., Kiron, D., and Buckley, N. (2018). Coming of Age Digitally. Learning, leadership and Legacy. Digital Business report by Deloitte and MIT Sloan Management Review. Available at: https://www2.deloitte.com/content/dam/Deloitte/mx/Documents/technology/Coming-of-age-digitally.pdf

Lahiri, G., Schwartz, J., and Volini, E. (2018). The rise of the social enterprise 2018. Deloitte Global Human Capital Trends. Available at: https://www2.deloitte.com/content/dam/insights/us/articles/HCTrends2018/2018-HCtrends_Rise-of-the-social-enterprise.pdf

Lahiri, G., Schwartz, J., and Volini, E. (2018). The symphonic C-suite: Teams leading teams 2018 Global Human Capital Trends. Deloitte Global Human Capital Trends. Available at: https://www2.deloitte.com/us/en/insights/focus/human-capital-trends/2018/senior-leadership-c-suite-collaboration.html